GCSE Edexcel Religious Studies
Christianity, Roman Catholic Christianity and Mark's Gospel
(Units 9, 10 and 16)
The Revision Guide

Want to hear the **bad news**? There's an awful lot of heavy-going
stuff they expect you to learn for GCSE Religious Studies.

Want to hear the **good news**? Good old CGP have got it all covered!
We've produced this brilliant book, with all the key concepts explained
in clear, simple English so you can understand it — and remember it.

And then, in the spirit of going the extra mile, we've put in
a smattering of not-so-serious bits to try and make the
whole experience at least partly entertaining for you.

We've done all we can — the rest is up to you.

What CGP is all about

Our sole aim here at CGP is to produce the highest quality
books — carefully written, immaculately presented and
dangerously close to being funny.

Then we work our socks off to get them out to you
— at the cheapest possible prices.

Contents

Section Five — Unit 16: Mark's Gospel

Bible References

References from the Bible always go in the order: **Book Chapter:Verse(s)**. So whenever you see something like: **Mark 3:5-6**, it means it's from the book of Mark, Chapter 3, Verses 5-6.

Published by Coordination Group Publications Ltd

Editors:
Luke von Kotze, Andy Park, Julie Wakeling

Contributors:
Maria Amayuelas-Tann, Jill Hudson

ISBN: 978 1 84762 302 7

With thanks to Mary Falkner and Karen Gascoigne for the proofreading.
With thanks to Laura Phillips for the copyright research.

Biblical quotations taken from the HOLY BIBLE, NEW INTERNATIONAL VERSION
Copyright © 1973, 1978, 1984 by International Bible Society
All rights reserved.
"NIV" is a registered trademark of the International Bible Society.
UK trademark number 1448790

Photograph on page 9 reproduced by permission of Rex Features.

With thanks to Enid Thompson for the church photos on pages 16 and 17.

Groovy website: www.cgpbooks.co.uk

Jolly bits of clipart from CorelDRAW®

Printed by Elanders Hindson Ltd, Newcastle upon Tyne

Based on the classic CGP style created by Richard Parsons.

Your Opinions Matter

Welcome to Religious Studies — it may be <u>a little bit different</u> from the subjects you've studied before. The first four sections of this book cover the <u>Christianity</u> and <u>Roman Catholicism</u> Units (that's half of the full course GCSE, or the whole of the short course GCSE). The last section's just for people taking the <u>Mark's Gospel</u> Unit. You get lots of <u>options</u> for RS, so make sure you've got the right book before you start.

In RS you get Marks for More than just Knowledge

In GCSE Religious Studies there are two 'assessment objectives' — these are the skills you'll need to show to get marks in the exams. You get <u>half</u> your marks for each.

> 1) The first gives you marks for <u>describing</u> and <u>explaining</u> what you <u>know</u>.
> 2) The second gives you marks for making <u>arguments</u> backed up with well-thought-out <u>reasoning</u> — and for <u>understanding</u> and <u>explaining</u> other people's opinions.

What You Think Matters...

1) So unlike most of the other subjects you might have exams on (such as maths), in RS you're supposed to <u>think</u> about what you're learning and come to your own <u>conclusions</u>.
2) A lot of the topics you study are pretty controversial — such as the authority of the Church. In RS you have to decide where <u>you</u> stand on these <u>difficult issues</u>.
3) In fact, being able to give reasoned <u>opinions</u> will count for <u>half</u> your <u>marks</u>.

In my opinion —
that is an awesome hat.

...But You've Still Got a Lot to Learn

1) Unfortunately, you can't just weigh in with opinions based on how you feel that afternoon. In the exam you have to <u>back up</u> what you say with <u>reasons</u>. Those reasons will be what you've <u>learnt</u> during the course.
2) You'll also need to know the <u>reasons</u> why some people might <u>disagree</u> with you. In other words, you'll have to present <u>both sides</u> of an argument.
3) And don't forget, the other half of your marks comes from just <u>knowing things</u>. As much as you need to be able to argue, you'll still need to learn all the basics — what things <u>mean</u> and what different people <u>believe</u>.

There'll be Fact Questions and Opinion Questions

So in the exam you'll get questions like:

> What is transubstantiation?

For these you have to give the definitions of the words you've learnt. There's a <u>glossary</u> in the back that should help you learn them.

As well as questions like:

> Do you think Christians should pray to Mary? Give two reasons for your point of view.

For which you'll need to give your own <u>opinion</u> — backed up with reasons.

And some like:

> Explain what Christians believe about the Trinity.

For these you'll need to give <u>details</u> about Christian beliefs and practices.

And some questions will ask you to: Give reasons why some people may disagree with you.

This means for each topic you're going to have to:

> 1) <u>Learn</u> the <u>facts</u>.
> 2) Work out what <u>you think</u> and <u>why</u>.
> 3) Learn <u>why</u> people might <u>disagree</u> with you.

What do you think of it so far?

It turns out that you have to do twice as much as you might have thought. First you've got to commit each topic to memory, and then you have to figure out what your take on it is. I guess in some ways it's unavoidable, given that this course is about what people <u>believe</u>. And I believe it's about time for some Religious Studies — oh yes.

The Nature of God

Worship offered to <u>Jesus</u> is what <u>distinguishes Christianity</u> from all <u>other monotheistic</u> (one-god) religions.

Christians **Believe in God as** <u>Unity</u> **and** <u>Trinity</u>

1) <u>Christians</u> believe in <u>one God</u> — God as <u>Unity</u>.

2) They believe that God is <u>omnipotent</u> (all-powerful), <u>omnipresent</u> (everywhere) and <u>omniscient</u> (all-knowing), that God is <u>divine</u>, <u>supreme</u>, <u>totally good</u> and <u>totally perfect</u>, and that God has given us <u>free will</u>.

However, many Christians believe that our lives are <u>predestined</u> — we control <u>individual actions</u>, but not the <u>ultimate outcome</u> of our lives.

3) Christians <u>also</u> believe in the <u>Trinity</u>...

The <u>Trinity</u> **is Explained Nicely in the** <u>Nicene Creed</u>

no pun intended...

1) The <u>Christian</u> idea of the <u>Trinity</u> is perhaps best expressed in the <u>Nicene Creed</u>:

> *"We believe in one God, the Father, the almighty, maker of heaven and earth... We believe in one Lord, Jesus Christ, the only son of God... Of one being with the Father... We believe in the Holy Spirit... The giver of life... Who proceeds from the Father and the Son..."*

2) Christians might describe the <u>Father</u> as the <u>creator</u> and <u>judge</u>, the <u>Son</u> (Jesus) as the <u>human incarnation</u> of God (and the <u>Messiah</u>, or saviour), and the <u>Holy Spirit</u> as the <u>presence of God</u> in the world — inspiring, guiding and comforting them.

The <u>Apostles' Creed</u> **— a Summary of the Christian Faith**

The <u>Apostles' Creed</u> summarises the basic Christian teachings about Jesus: *'Creed' means a statement of religious beliefs.*

① **Jesus is the Christ**   'Christ' isn't a surname — it means the same as '<u>Messiah</u>', i.e. '<u>Anointed One of God</u>'.

② **The Incarnation**   This was the act by which <u>God</u> became a <u>human being</u>. Note that Christians don't believe Jesus was 'half God and half man' — he was <u>fully both</u>.

③ **The Virgin Birth**   The Gospels say that Jesus was born of a <u>virgin</u> — Mary became pregnant through the <u>influence</u> of the <u>Holy Spirit</u>. This is why Christians say "God's Son", or "God the Son".

④ **The Crucifixion**   It was Jesus's death on the cross which won his people <u>forgiveness</u> of sin.

⑤ **The Resurrection**   Jesus rose from the dead on Easter Day, and is still alive <u>today</u>.

⑥ **The Ascension**   After the resurrection Jesus '<u>ascended into Heaven</u>' (not necessarily 'in the sky').

1) The Apostles' Creed also includes important teaching about <u>God the Father</u> and the <u>Holy Spirit</u>.

2) Although Christians believe in only one God, this God exists in three forms — God the <u>Father</u>, God the <u>Son</u> and God the <u>Holy Spirit</u>. Together, these three make up the <u>Trinity</u>.

3) The Holy Spirit is God's <u>influence</u> in the world, and is often pictured as <u>fire</u>, or as a <u>dove</u>, or thought of as a <u>wind</u>.

After the <u>Ascension</u>, God sent his Spirit down upon Jesus's followers in 'tongues of fire'.

At Jesus's <u>baptism</u> the Spirit descended on him in the form of a dove.

For Christians, the statements in the creeds are matters of <u>faith</u> — <u>firmly-held beliefs</u>, without (and without need for) logical proof.

The nature of God — well I thought I'd ease you in gently...

There's a lot of big ideas on this page, and it's really important that you get your head round them. Christians believe in <u>one God</u> who exists as <u>three persons</u> — the Father, the Son (Jesus) and the Holy Spirit. They believe that Jesus was <u>fully God</u> and <u>fully human</u>, that he died, was resurrected and <u>still lives</u> in heaven.

The Trinity

So, back to this Trinity business. It's really important to Christians, so you'd best know a bit more about it.

Christians Believe in the Father...

> "In the beginning God created the heavens and the earth." Genesis 1:1

1) For many Christians, God the Father is the God of the Old Testament.
2) The title 'Father' is a mark of respect for God, and is used by Jesus in the Gospels: "...when you pray... pray to your Father, who is unseen. Then your Father, who sees what is done in secret, will reward you." (Matthew 6:6).
3) In Genesis 1, the Bible describes God as the Creator of heaven and earth, who created the world in six days. Some Christians believe this account literally, while others think that it should be understood symbolically.
4) To most Christians, belief in God as the Creator is important as it means that the world itself must be a good thing since he chose to create it, and that life is God's gift to us. Some Christians take their belief in the Creator to mean that we have a responsibility to look after the environment, as it was made for us.
5) Many Christian traditions teach that God the Father will be our Judge after death. Since Christians believe God is all-knowing, everything they say, do or think is important as it will be judged by God.

...the Son...

1) Christians believe that Jesus is the incarnation of God in human form, and that God sending Jesus down to us shows how much he loves the world.
2) They believe Jesus is the Christ or Messiah ('anointed one') prophesied by Isaiah in the Old Testament.
3) Christians believe that Jesus provides a model for Christian behaviour in obedience to God the Father. The Gospels contain a record of his life and teachings, and are an important source of guidance for Christians on how they should live their lives.
4) Jesus is sometimes described as the 'lamb of God'. This is a reference to the lambs offered as sacrifices to God in the Jewish Temple. Christ is seen as a sacrifice on behalf of all humanity.

Jesus Offers Christians Salvation from Sin
Christians believe that through his suffering and death, Jesus won forgiveness for the sins of all people. They believe that Jesus was perfect (without sin), but that God placed all the sins of the world on him at his crucifixion: "...the LORD has laid on him the iniquity of us all." (Isaiah 53:6). Christianity teaches that his sacrifice paid for our sins, so long as we have faith in him (more about this on the next page). Christians believe that Christ's victory over the power of sin and death was revealed in his resurrection.

As Jesus suffered, many Christians believe they have a duty to help those who are suffering.

...and the Holy Spirit

1) Christians believe that the Holy Spirit is the presence of God in the world, who descended on Christ's disciples after his Ascension and continues to guide the actions of the Church.
2) Some Christians feel that the Holy Spirit also guides them personally in being good Christians.
3) Charismatic Christians believe that the Holy Spirit can descend on them during worship, just as with Christ's disciples. For example they might begin to 'speak in tongues' (unknown languages) or shake uncontrollably.
4) Different beliefs about the Holy Spirit are what initially separated the Orthodox and the Roman Catholic Churches during the Great Schism. Catholics (and from them Protestants) believe that the Holy Spirit descended from God the Father and God the Son, whereas the Orthodox Christians believe that the Holy Spirit is the product of the God the Father alone.
5) The Holy Spirit is often represented by a dove.
6) For Roman Catholics the most important action of the Holy Spirit is in guiding the Church. They believe that the Holy Spirit is how God continues to influence history through the Church.

Roman Catholic beliefs about the Trinity are detailed in the catechism — a series of statements laying down the official teachings of the Church.

Three into one doesn't go in maths — but this is RS...

Remember, this stuff about the Trinity doesn't mean that Christians believe in three Gods — they're just different forms of the same God. It's a bit like the way water can be steam, ice or, well, water...

4

Love and the Christian Faith

Love is central to the Christian faith.

God showed his Love by Sending Jesus

One of the most frequently quoted verses from the Bible is:

> "For God so loved the world that he gave his one and only Son, that whoever believes in him shall not perish but have eternal life." John 3:16

1) Christians believe that God expressed his love for us by sending us his son — who, although he was perfect, was punished so that our sins could be forgiven (see p.3).
2) This reconciliation between God and humanity is known as the atonement.
3) Christians believe that we must trust and love God and accept Christ as our saviour.
4) Then if we repent of our sins (are sorry, seek forgiveness and try hard not to repeat them) we will be forgiven. And doing so will lead to our salvation — we will be accepted into eternal life.

Jesus Taught Us Not Just to Respect — but to Love

1) Jesus's Jewish opponents often accused him of breaking religious laws — he healed people on the Sabbath when Jews were not supposed to do any work, for example.

But Jesus said he wasn't trying to undermine the law — "Do not think that I have come to abolish the Law or the Prophets; I have not come to abolish them but to fulfil them." Matthew 5:17.

2) Jesus thought the Jewish authorities had missed the point of God's Law, and that the 'spirit' of the law was more important than the 'letter'. He believed that if you were a good person, you'd do good things.
3) In fact, he taught that your motivation was even more important than your actions — being angry with someone could be just as bad as killing them (Matthew 5:21-22).
4) For Jesus, respect wasn't enough — he wanted his followers to love. When asked which was the most important commandment in Judaism (i.e. all the laws given to the Jews in the first five books of the Bible), he gave a pretty neat answer which summed up his beliefs...

> "'The most important one,' answered Jesus, 'is this... Love the Lord your God with all your heart and with all your soul and with all your mind and with all your strength. The second is this: Love your neighbour as yourself.'" Mark 12:29-31

Love is a Key Concept in Christianity

Love is what the Christian faith is all about, but this isn't always as simple as it might seem. Christians have developed the concept of agape — a selfless love, unconditional, always serving and always caring.

In Matthew 25:31-46, Jesus talks of separating out those who will be saved from those who won't. He explains that salvation will come to those who demonstrate love by helping people in need:

> "For I was hungry and you gave me something to eat, I was thirsty and you gave me something to drink, I was a stranger and you invited me in... I tell you the truth, whatever you did for one of the least of these brothers of mine, you did for me." Matthew 25:35-40

In essence Jesus asks us to love those in need as if they were him.

1) In another example, a man asks Jesus who his 'neighbour' is, since he's commanded to 'love his neighbour'. Jesus replies with the parable of the Good Samaritan (Luke 10:25-37). It isn't the religious leaders of the Jewish community, but the Samaritan, a member of an ethnic and religious group separate from the Jews and looked down on by many at the time, who provides the model of religious love.
2) This parable argues that compassion — the feeling of pity for and the desire to help those who suffer — is more important to God than being high up in the religious hierarchy.

The Good Samaritan — what a nice bloke...

Respect and love are the basic principles of Christianity — but that doesn't mean that they can provide easy answers to complex questions. However, they give you a place to start thinking, which can sometimes help.

Love and the Christian Faith

Christians believe that love is all-important, and they express this in a number of different ways.

Religious Communities Worship Full Time

Religious communities express their love of God by fully committing to a life of worship.
Members of religious communities will usually make vows dedicating their lives to God (a bit like in a marriage).

Members of most religious orders take three vows

Poverty — Members aren't allowed personal possessions. These are given to the community or the poor.
Chastity — Members abstain from sexual relationships to better focus on a life of prayer.
Obedience — Members follow the rules of the community, and promise to obey superiors in the order.

There are two main types of religious community

Contemplative Orders — dedicate their lives to prayer. Enclosed (or cloistered) orders, such as Cistercians, live within the confines of the religious community.
Apostolic Orders — live an active life by serving in the 'world'. Examples include the Sisters of Mercy who are involved in teaching, and caring for the sick.

I like to be alone, so I support Millom Athletic.

Religious Communities Express their Love of God...

1) Those in contemplative orders aim to remove themselves from the world and dedicate their lives to God through prayer, and to living together in peace.
2) Monks and nuns pray at a number of specific times during the day — starting from early in the morning (around 4:30 a.m.) through into the late evening. The rest of their time will usually be spent studying scripture or working — many religious orders make things to sell to fund the community.
3) Members of apostolic orders also dedicate time to prayer and study — but this fits into their work 'in the world' rather than being their sole focus.
4) Some Protestants don't agree with religious communities based on vows, since this idea isn't mentioned in the Bible. So most are Roman Catholic, but some Protestant religious orders do exist.

...and Other People

1) Those in apostolic orders go out into the community to try to help people and to advance their faith. For example, the Roman Catholic Society of Jesus (Jesuits) are famous for their work in education.
2) Mother Teresa was a Roman Catholic nun who founded the Order of the Missionaries of Charity in Calcutta, India. The nuns of her order now work to relieve the suffering of the poor all over the world. She said that it isn't what you do for God that counts, but how much love you pour into it.
3) Members of contemplative orders will pray for other people and offer spiritual guidance to visitors.

Love of God and Others is also Seen in Local Churches

1) Most local churches try to take an active role in the community.
2) A church's main function is to help its congregation express their love of God through regular religious services for people in their local area (parishioners).
3) Some local churches demonstrate their love for others by getting involved in campaigns on social issues, e.g. by raising money to help the poor and underpriviliged, or encouraging people to buy Fair Trade products.
4) Many churches have youth groups and Sunday Schools to encourage young people to get involved in the Church and its activities.

Love never ends — I am the walrus, goo, goo, ga joob...

If you look at a notice board in your town, or by one of your local churches, you'll see that churches get involved in all sorts of activities: church choirs, coffee mornings, Bible study groups, fund-raising... all to express love of God and of other people. Who'd have thought a jumble sale could be an expression of love.

Practice Questions

Here endeth the first section. There's quite a lot of big stuff to take in here, so make sure you go through the section as many times as it takes for you to understand and remember it all.

Just to help that process along, here are some practice questions for you. They're in the same kind of format you'll find in the exam. Try to answer all the questions, then check back through the section for the ones you couldn't answer. Then try the questions again. If you get stuck on the wordy questions, there are some exam help pages at the back of the book to give you a few pointers. Off you go then...

1) What is:
   a) monotheism?
   b) a creed?
   c) the Incarnation?
   d) the Virgin Birth?
   e) faith?
   f) the catechism?
   g) the Atonement?
   h) repentance?
   i) salvation?
   j) compassion?

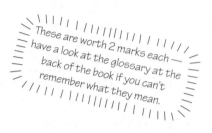
These are worth 2 marks each — have a look at the glossary at the back of the book if you can't remember what they mean.

2) For each of the following questions, give <u>two</u> reasons for your point of view.
   a) Do you think God should be called the Creator?
   b) Do you think being compassionate is the most important quality for a Christian?
   c) Do you think Christians should be more concerned with their motivations or their actions?
   d) Do you think Christian religious communities have a positive impact on the world?

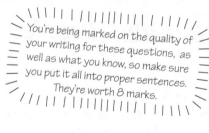
Make sure you back up each reason with some evidence — you can get up to 4 marks for these questions.

3) For these questions, take extra care with your spelling, punctuation and grammar, and express yourself as clearly as possible.
   a) Explain what Christians believe about the Trinity.
   b) Explain why Christians think love is important.
   c) Explain what Christians believe about salvation.
   d) Explain why some Christians think charity work is an important expression of their faith.

You're being marked on the quality of your writing for these questions, as well as what you know, so make sure you put it all into proper sentences. They're worth 8 marks.

4) Read the following statements:
   a) "God cannot be three and one at the same time."
   b) "To be a Christian you have to go out and help people."
   c) "You cannot focus on a love of God and a love of other people at the same time."
   d) "Churches should focus on helping their own followers."
   For each statement:
   (i) Do you agree? Give reasons for your opinion.
   (ii) Give reasons why some people may disagree with you.
   In your answers you should refer to Christianity/Roman Catholic Christianity.

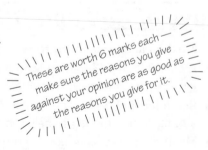
These are worth 6 marks each — make sure the reasons you give against your opinion are as good as the reasons you give for it.

The Bible

The <u>Bible</u> is a <u>collection</u> of books in different styles and languages written over a period of about 1000 years. It's also the Christian <u>Scriptures</u> — meaning that for Christians, it's <u>sacred</u>.

The Bible — the Old and New Testaments

The Bible's divided into 2 main parts — the <u>Old</u> and <u>New Testaments</u>:

THE OLD TESTAMENT

The Old Testament is the <u>Jewish Scriptures</u> (i.e. it's considered sacred by Jews). Written in Hebrew and Aramaic, its 39 books include the <u>Creation</u> story, the books of the Law (<u>Torah</u>), the <u>10 Commandments</u>, various <u>histories</u> of Ancient Israel, <u>prophecy</u>, <u>poetry</u> and <u>psalms</u>.

THE NEW TESTAMENT

The New Testament is the specifically <u>Christian</u> part of the Bible. Written in Greek in the 1st Century CE, its 27 books include the <u>4 Gospels</u>, the <u>Acts</u> of the Apostles (describing the early years of Christianity), 13 <u>letters</u> by St Paul (giving advice about the Christian life), 8 letters by other early Christian leaders, and the <u>Revelation of St John</u> — an apocalyptic vision.

The 4 Gospels are Matthew, Mark, Luke (called the <u>Synoptic Gospels</u>, as they are all very similar stories of Jesus), and John (which portrays Jesus in a very different way).
The word 'Gospel' means 'good news', and the Gospels tell the good news about Jesus Christ.

The Bible is used as a Christian Faith Guidebook

Christians accept the Bible as <u>authoritative</u> in forming their beliefs and guiding their actions.

1) Christians believe the Bible offers directions for living a <u>moral</u> life. It presents Jesus Christ as our example for <u>godly</u> living, and teaches that we best love <u>God</u> by showing love to <u>others</u>.

2) Both the Old and New Testaments (but especially the New) include <u>rituals</u> for <u>worship</u>, large parts of which are still included in <u>modern</u> worship services (e.g. <u>Holy Communion</u> and <u>baptism</u>).

3) The practices of the Roman Catholic Church are based largely on the <u>Scriptures</u>, but Catholic <u>tradition</u> and the <u>Magisterium</u> (see p.10) are also very important. Protestant Churches claim their authority mainly from the Scriptures.

4) Different groups of Christians <u>interpret</u> the Bible in different ways:

① **Literalism** Many Christians believe that pretty well everything in the Bible is <u>literally</u> true, e.g. Jesus really did 'walk on water'.

Some people argue that there are <u>contradictions</u> in the Bible, and so it's impossible for everything to be <u>literally</u> true.

② **Fundamentalism** This is a form of literalism. Fundamentalists believe that it's wrong to <u>question</u> anything in the Bible, since it is the <u>direct word</u> of God.

③ **Conservative View** This view is probably the most common among Christians. They believe that the Bible was <u>inspired</u> by God but not dictated — the writers' own interests also come through. Readers must use their intelligence and the guidance of the Holy Spirit in order to understand the writers' intentions.

④ **Liberal View** Liberals believe that pretty well everything in the Bible can be interpreted '<u>symbolically</u>', e.g. Jesus didn't really 'walk on water' — the story has some other 'spiritual' meaning.

The Bible has been Influential for Centuries

1) There are many different <u>versions</u> of the Bible in use today, and loads of <u>translations</u> into different languages.

2) The <u>Gospels</u> (which contain the teachings of Jesus) are <u>central</u> to the Christian faith.

3) Christians often meet to <u>study</u> the Bible and to <u>pray</u>, and it's also read for <u>guidance</u>, or as an act of <u>devotion</u> to God.

The Bible — sells more than any revision guide...

The Bible has profoundly affected <u>countless</u> lives (e.g. the saints, missionaries, campaigners for social change), and arguments over its interpretation continue to be a <u>legal</u> matter in some countries — e.g. courts in the USA have had to legislate recently on whether schools should teach the Bible's Creation story as <u>fact</u> or <u>fable</u>.

Christian Traditions and the Virgin Mary

There are significant variations among Christians' beliefs, but they share some kind of 'relationship with Christ'.

Three Main Traditions — Roman Catholic, Orthodox and Protestant

There have been a couple of major splits in the history of the Christian Church.

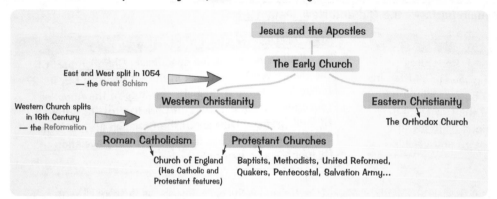

Jesus and the Apostles

The Early Church

East and West split in 1054 — the Great Schism

Western Christianity

Eastern Christianity
The Orthodox Church

Western Church splits in 16th Century — the Reformation

Roman Catholicism

Protestant Churches

Church of England (Has Catholic and Protestant features)

Baptists, Methodists, United Reformed, Quakers, Pentecostal, Salvation Army...

In the Great Schism, the Pope and the Orthodox Patriarch excommunicated each other from their churches.

The Reformation began when Martin Luther challenged the authority of the Pope.

Roman Catholics
1) Roman Catholics are all those Christians who accept the authority of the Pope. They are the largest Christian group in the world.
2) They believe in the 7 sacraments as 'vehicles of God's grace' (see page 13).
3) They respect the authority of the Bible, Church tradition and the Magisterium (p.10).

Protestants
1) Protestants base their beliefs and practices on the ideas of the Reformation.
2) The Reformers stressed the importance of the Bible rather than Church tradition or the teachings of the Pope.

The Church of England has both Roman Catholic and Protestant features. Anglicanism is the worldwide 'communion' of churches in fellowship with the parent Church of England.

3) Members of the Protestant clergy are usually referred to as ministers.
4) The different groupings within Protestantism are known as denominations. In England and Wales, Protestant denominations that are not part of the 'Anglican Communion' are often called 'Nonconformists'. These include Methodists, Baptists, Pentecostals, The Society of Friends (Quakers) and the Salvation Army.

Orthodox Christians
1) Orthodox Christians are found mainly in Eastern Europe, Russia and Greece.
2) They believe that their clergy are in direct succession from the Apostles (see p.10).
3) They also have 7 sacraments, and honour (but don't worship) icons — pictures of saints.

The Different Traditions have Different Beliefs about Mary

1) Not only is Mary important to Christians because she gave birth to Jesus, she is seen as the model for Christian living, because she cooperated fully with God's will.

2) Roman Catholicism teaches that she was born without original sin, meaning she had none of the flaws that all other humans have — this is known as the Immaculate Conception.

3) Roman Catholic and Orthodox Christians also believe she remained a virgin all her life, and after she died she was taken up to Heaven in the Assumption. They don't believe that Mary died a normal death — instead she's believed to have been taken directly up to Heaven.

4) Catholics don't worship Mary, but they do pray to her and ask her to pray for them (for example in the 'Ave Maria/Hail Mary'). She is also known as 'Mother of God'.

5) Protestants generally believe that Mary is worthy of great respect. But they don't believe in praying to her, as they see this as a form of idolatry — i.e. worshipping something other than God.

6) Protestants also reject the ideas of Immaculate Conception and the Assumption, as they're not in the Bible.

Movers and Shakers — Cockney rhyming slang for Quakers... (maybe)

There are at least 20,800 denominations worldwide, so don't think that the above list is all there is to know. But at the same time, don't feel as though you need to know everything about all 20,800 — that would be a pretty tough assignment. Though not for God, obviously, because he's omniscient.

The Role of the Church

The 'Church' traces its roots back to its founder, Jesus Christ. It's basically a community of believers. Those who profess faith in Jesus as God's promised Messiah become part of that community.

The Church — More than a Building

1) The mission of the Church is to expand the community of Christian believers and to help care for those who are already part of the community.

2) The Church teaches that Jesus Christ is our Saviour (see p.3-4), and that we can be saved by becoming his disciples. Being a disciple is more than just believing in Jesus — the Church teaches that you have to actively follow him by keeping his commandments and trying to be a good person.

3) Many Christians believe that being a member of the Church is necessary for salvation — that you can't win a place in heaven just by performing good deeds. But the Roman Catholic catechism states that someone who's never heard the Gospels can still find salvation through God's mercy.

4) The ceremony of baptism welcomes people into the Church. Roman Catholics believe that baptism is a sacrament (see p.13), and that some form of baptism is necessary to "enter the Kingdom of God".

Saint Paul Called the Church the Body of Christ

1) St Paul taught that the community of believers was the "Body of Christ" on Earth, with Christ as its head.

2) Christians who have died remain part of the faith community. The Church, made up of all Christians living or dead, is referred to as the Communion of Saints.

3) Christians believe the Church is 'holy' — sacred or belonging to God.

4) Despite its fragmentation into various traditions and denominations, the Church claims a spiritual unity. The word 'catholic' (small 'c') meaning universal is used to describe the community of all Christian believers.

The Church has Various Functions in the Community

Most communities in the UK have access to at least one church. The role and function of local church communities is to put the Christian faith into action. They do this in the following ways:

i) By providing a regular pattern of worship — most churches hold a Sunday service every week, and may also have other acts of communal worship throughout the week.

ii) By providing 'rites of passage' — e.g. baptisms, confirmations, weddings, funerals...

iii) By teaching Christian beliefs as part of regular services, Sunday schools or Bible classes.

iv) By ministering to the sick, e.g. visiting and praying for parishioners in hospital.

v) By supporting groups that campaign for justice and peace.

The Roman Catholic Church has a Powerful Influence

The Pope has a massive influence over Roman Catholics — e.g. over the issues of abortion and contraception.

Mimmo Chianura/Rex Features

1) The teachings of the Roman Catholic Church on moral issues (such as abortion, sexuality and social responsibility) continue to have a strong influence on its followers.

2) Church leaders are held in respect, and their pronouncements are adhered to by faithful followers.

3) The Church also offers guidance to those who believe they may be called by God into a specific vocation e.g. the ordained ministry.

4) The Church also influences social and political development all around the world, through its involvement in peace and justice movements.

Churches — 'big-C' are communities, 'little-c' are buildings...

Yep — so don't go assuming that when the exam asks a question about the Church, it's talking about that building down the road that rings its bells once a week. There's a wee bit more to it than that.

The Authority of the Church

For Roman Catholics, the only authority higher than the Church is God.

For Roman Catholics, the Church is the Supreme Authority

Roman Catholics consider the authority of the Church to be absolute on matters of faith.
This position of power is based on three main beliefs.

The Apostolic Tradition

'Apostolic' just means 'of, or relating to the Apostles'.
For Roman Catholics, the Church's link to the Apostles is very important.

1) The Apostolic Tradition is a body of teachings and ritual practices, which the Roman Catholic Church believe was handed down through the early Church from the Apostles.

2) The Gospel authors themselves explain that they do not provide a complete record of Jesus's life and teaching: *"Jesus did many other things as well. If every one of them were written down, I suppose that even the whole world would not have room for the books that would be written."* (John 21:25).

3) Catholics believe this means that the traditions of the Church have as important a role to play in true Christian faith as the Bible — this means that not everything that Catholics believe will necessarily be taken from the Bible. In contrast, most Protestant denominations try to base everything on scripture.

The Apostolic Succession

1) The Apostolic Succession is what Catholics believe makes a Church. It's the fact that new bishops were ordained by bishops who were ordained by bishops, going back in direct succession to the original Apostles as chosen by Christ.

Churches that believe they were originally founded by the Apostles describe themselves as apostolic.

2) This fact is so important that the Catholic Church does not recognise Protestant Churches as true Churches because of their break with this succession.

3) The Pope is believed to be a direct successor of St Peter — 'the first Pope'. Catholics view the Pope as the most important figure in the Church because Christ singled out St Peter: *"And I tell you that you are Peter, and on this rock I will build my church, and the gates of Hades will not overcome it."* (Matthew 16:18)

The Magisterium

1) The Magisterium is the authority of the Pope and his bishops to teach correctly in all matters of faith and morals. Roman Catholics believe this authority is given by the Holy Spirit. The Church has the final say in the interpretation of scripture and tradition.

2) When the Pope and the bishops agree on a point of doctrine it becomes part of official Church teaching — and Catholics are then supposed not only to follow the teaching, but also to believe in it fully.

3) The Pope can make official statements on his own on questions of faith and morals and these are believed to be infallible (they can't be wrong), but this doesn't happen very often — the last time was in 1950.

4) The firm beliefs of the Catholic Church are known as dogmas.
Most of them are set out in the Roman Catholic catechism (see p.3)

Unit 10: RC only

Protestant Churches have less Authority

1) Different Protestant Churches hold different views on the importance of Church hierarchy.

2) For example, Congregationalists believe each individual church is responsible for its own organisation. But Presbyterians send elders from each church to form councils which have authority over the churches.

3) Protestants tend to place far greater emphasis on a believer's own faith and understanding of the Bible according to their own conscience — and far less on the authority and teachings of the Church. This is one of the reasons why there are so many different Protestant denominations, as people often left old Churches and set up new ones, because they disagreed on an aspect of Church teaching.

This page is supremely authoritative...

Arguments about the importance and authority of the Church played a key part in the Reformation — when the Protestants split from the Roman Catholic Church. So Protestants will have very different views on this stuff from Catholics. Make sure you know both sides, so you can answer a question about it in the exam.

The Role of the Clergy

This is a page full of <u>bishops</u> and <u>priests</u> and stuff.

The <u>Roman Catholic</u> Church has a <u>Hierarchy...</u>

The Roman Catholic Church is arranged in a <u>hierarchy</u>, with the Pope at the top.

Pope

Cardinals

Bishops

Priests

Laity

THE POPE — The <u>Bishop of Rome</u> and head of the worldwide Roman Catholic Church. Jesus is believed to have chosen St Peter as the first Pope, and the current Pope is his spiritual descendant. On matters of faith and morals, the Pope is regarded as <u>infallible</u>, and his teachings are <u>binding</u> on all Roman Catholics (see also page 10). The office of the Pope is known as the <u>papacy</u>.

CARDINALS — The highest rank of bishop next to the Pope. They're appointed by the Pope, and act as his <u>advisors</u>. In turn, they're responsible for electing the Pope's <u>successor</u>.

BISHOPS — Bishops are appointed by the Pope — they each have responsibility for the churches in their <u>diocese</u> (a district made up of several parishes).

PRIESTS — A priest is the head of an individual <u>parish</u> (an area served by a local church). Priests are in charge of Catholic worship and education in their parish.

LAITY — all the <u>non-ordained</u> members of the Roman Catholic Church.

1) The office of priest (and those above it in the hierarchy) can be held by men (and <u>only</u> men) who have been <u>ordained</u>, i.e. officially admitted into the <u>clergy</u>. The rite of ordination is one of the seven <u>sacraments</u> (see p.13), and it can only be performed by a <u>bishop</u>. A <u>deacon</u> is also an ordained minister (see p.20).

2) A Roman Catholic <u>priest</u> has a number of <u>roles</u> within the parish. His main roles are to lead the celebration of the <u>Mass</u> (only a priest or bishop can perform the Liturgy of the Eucharist, see p.14) and to hear <u>confession</u> (see p.13). It's also his job to <u>preach</u> the Gospel, administer the <u>sacraments</u> of baptism, marriage and anointing the sick (see p.13) and to offer <u>support</u> and <u>guidance</u> to the people of the parish.

...and so do the <u>Protestant</u> and <u>Orthodox</u> Churches

1) The <u>Anglican Church</u> also has a hierarchy of priests and bishops, with the Archbishop of Canterbury (the head bishop of the Church of England) at the top.

2) Anglican priests traditionally have a <u>similar</u> role to Roman Catholic priests in the parish, but the Church of England is increasingly encouraging <u>lay ministry</u>. Anglican priests <u>don't</u> hear confession.

Lay ministers are non-ordained church members who are trained to perform certain duties, e.g. visiting the sick or leading worship.

3) In the Presbyterian Church, <u>presbyters</u> (or elders) are church leaders with the specific responsibility of <u>preaching</u> and teaching from the Bible. They're appointed by the local congregation and answerable to the church members when they meet.

4) In the Orthodox Church, <u>patriarchs</u> are at the head of each regional church, with the Patriarch of Constantinople (or Istanbul) being the 'first among equals'. Men can become Orthodox priests at 30.

Roman Catholic <u>Priests must be Celibate</u>

1) In the Catholic Church, to become a <u>priest</u> a man has to be <u>unmarried</u> and <u>stay celibate</u> (not have <u>sex</u>). Catholics believe that this allows priests to focus fully on their <u>spiritual duties</u>.

2) They base this on the teachings of <u>Paul</u> that *"It is good for a man not to marry"* (1 Corinthians 7:1) and Jesus's remark that some *"have renounced marriage because of the kingdom of heaven"* (Matthew 19:12).

3) In recent years there has been a <u>fall</u> in the number of men wanting to become priests. Some Catholics <u>blame</u> this on the celibacy rule.

4) Protestants argue that celibacy is <u>not stated</u> as a qualification for priesthood in the Bible. Some have argued that celibacy is too difficult for many and so becomes a <u>distraction</u> rather than an aid to spiritual life.

5) Anglican priests and Protestant ministers are allowed to marry either before or after they're ordained. Some denominations <u>encourage</u> ministers to marry, to set a good example for the congregation.

6) In the <u>Orthodox</u> tradition married men can be ordained as priests (but not bishops) — but they can't get married once they've been ordained.

Practice Questions

There are plenty of different Christian traditions in this section to get to know and love — except they haven't always loved each other very much.

But that's the joy of RS — you have to learn what everybody believes and use that knowledge to answer questions like these. Answer all the questions you can, then check all the answers against the section. Repeat the above till you can get them all spot on without checking back.
Some Christians call this process 'revision'.

Oh, and if a question's marked Christianity, it's just for Unit 9: Christianity. If it's marked Roman Catholicism, it's just for Unit 10: Roman Catholicism. (Not rocket science, I know, but I thought I'd best say...)

1) What is meant by:
   a) the New Testament? *(Christianity)*
   b) the Old Testament? *(Christianity)*
   c) the Anglican Church?
   d) Nonconformist Churches?
   e) Orthodox Churches?
   f) catholic? *(Note the small 'c'.)*
   g) apostolic?
   h) the Magisterium? *(Roman Catholicism)*
   i) a bishop?
   j) the laity?
   k) the papacy?
   l) ordination?
   m) celibacy?

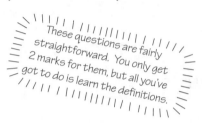
These questions are fairly straightforward. You only get 2 marks for them, but all you've got to do is learn the definitions.

2) For each of the following questions, give <u>two</u> reasons for your point of view.
   a) Do you think Christians should pray to Mary? *(Christianity)*
   b) Do you think being apostolic is important for a Church?
   c) Do you think Roman Catholics should follow the teachings of the Pope and bishops? *(Roman Catholicism)*
   d) Do you think it is important for a community to have a priest/minister?

4 marks each for these. You don't get marks for having the 'right' opinion — you get them for giving reasons backed up with good arguments.

3) For these questions, take extra care with your spelling, punctuation and grammar, and express yourself as clearly as possible.
   a) Explain why some Christians believe the Bible is the direct word of God and others do not. *(Christianity)*
   b) Explain why the Bible is important to Christians/Roman Catholics.
   c) Explain why Roman Catholics honour the Virgin Mary.
   d) Describe the role of a local church or priest in the community.
   e) Explain why Roman Catholics do not believe that the Bible is the only source of religious authority.

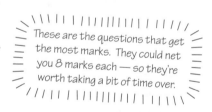
These are the questions that get the most marks. They could net you 8 marks each — so they're worth taking a bit of time over.

4) Read the following statements:
   a) "The Bible is too old to be of any value today."
   b) "Any Church that lacks the Apostolic Succession is not a real Church."
   c) "Priests should remain celibate."
   d) "Individual churches should be responsible for themselves."
   For each statement:
   (i) Do you agree? Give reasons for your opinion.
   (ii) Give reasons why some people may disagree with you.
   In your answers you should refer to Christianity/Roman Catholic Christianity.

These are worth 6 marks each, so you'll need a well-developed reason, or a number of reasons for each side of the argument.

The Seven Sacraments

Roman Catholic and Orthodox Churches believe in seven sacraments.

The Seven Sacraments — Vehicles of God's Grace

God is thought to communicate his grace (unearned favour) directly through sacraments, whether or not the recipient understands what it all means. The sacraments are:

> Some Protestants also accept baptism and Eucharist as sacraments.

1. **Baptism** — Baptism (see p.15) marks a person's official entry into the Church.

2. **Confirmation** — In this ceremony a Christian renews the vows made on his or her behalf at baptism.

3. **Reconciliation** — This involves confession of a sin, followed by contrition, penance and absolution.

4. **Eucharist** — In Holy Communion (see p.14), the believer receives Christ into him- or herself afresh.

5. **Ordination** — This is the rite in which people are made deacons, priests or bishops (see p.11).

6. **Marriage** — When a couple are joined in Holy Matrimony they receive a special blessing.

7. **Anointing of the Sick** — This may be for healing, or to prepare a dying person for his or her journey into the next life.

This is when a priest applies consecrated oil.

Confirmation helps Strengthen a Person's Faith

1) Most Churches have a Confirmation rite. For Roman Catholics, Orthodox Christians and some Anglicans, it is considered a sacrament. It is believed to strengthen the ties of the confirmed to the Church and to God.

2) In Catholic Confirmations, the bishop anoints the believer's forehead with holy oil called chrism. This oil has been consecrated (made holy) with a blessing from a bishop.

3) Catholics get confirmed around the age of seven, when they're old enough to understand what it means. They have to show that they understand their faith — usually by attending a course of religious instruction.

4) In the Catholic Church, only confirmed Church members can receive the Eucharist.

Reconciliation makes up for Sin

1) Reconciliation through confession is how Roman Catholics obtain forgiveness for the sins they commit.

2) Confession is where a believer admits to a priest any sinful things that they've done. To prepare for this, a believer must think seriously about the sins they've committed.

3) The priest will give a penance (a certain number of prayers to be said, or an action to be done) and will then pronounce absolution (God's forgiveness). For confession to be effective the believer needs to be genuinely sorry and make a commitment not to sin again — this is known as contrition.

4) Confession and reconciliation are important. All Catholics are supposed to confess at least once a year, but are recommended to do it more regularly. If a Catholic commits a serious (mortal) sin they should confess as soon as possible — Catholics believe that if they die unreconciled, they will go to Hell.

Catholics Believe in Anointing the Sick

1) Catholics believe in anointing the sick — this is where a priest or a bishop anoints a seriously unwell person with the oil of the sick (oil, usually scented with balsam, that has been blessed by a bishop).

2) If someone is facing death it will be administered as part of the Last Rites, along with a final confession and a final Eucharist (known as the viaticum).

3) Catholics believe that, through this sacrament, the Holy Spirit renews the sick person's faith and strength to cope with their illness and accept their suffering. The anointing is also believed to link the person's suffering to the suffering of Christ, allow their sins to be forgiven and to heal them, if that is God's will.

Big Cats Rarely Eat 'Orrible Maggoty Apples...

Try this way of remembering the initial letters of the seven sacraments. It's a good 'un.

Mass and the Eucharist

The <u>Mass</u> is the Roman Catholic service that includes the Eucharist (Holy Communion).

Holy Communion Commemorates the Last Supper

1) At the <u>Last Supper</u>, Jesus said that the bread and wine on the table represented his <u>body</u> and <u>blood</u>. The disciples were to eat and drink in remembrance of him whenever they ate together.

2) Virtually all Christians recognise the importance of <u>Holy Communion</u> (also called the <u>Eucharist</u>), but most see it as largely <u>commemorative</u> — it <u>reminds</u> worshippers of the Last Supper and Jesus's sacrifice.

3) However, Roman Catholics believe that the bread and wine actually <u>become</u> the body and blood of Christ, by the power of the Holy Spirit. This is known as <u>transubstantiation</u>, and it is through this that Jesus takes up <u>residence</u> in his people. This is why it's vital for Roman Catholics to attend Mass regularly.

There are Four Key Features of a Catholic Mass:

Penitential Rite

This is a <u>joint confession</u> of sin and a request for God's mercy and forgiveness in the form of a prayer said by the whole congregation. It's followed by the reciting of the '<u>Kyrie</u>' prayer, either in Greek or in English. "*Kyrie, eleison (Lord have mercy) Christe, eleison (Christ have mercy) Kyrie, eleison (Lord have mercy)*".

Liturgy of the Word

A '<u>liturgy</u>' is a well-defined <u>pattern</u> of rituals, set prayers and readings.

The penitential rite is followed by the <u>liturgy of the word</u>. This consists of readings from scripture, usually including a section from one of the Gospels, followed by a <u>homily</u> (a short sermon based on the readings). This is followed by a joint recitation of either the <u>Nicene Creed</u> or the <u>Apostles' Creed</u> (see p.2).

Liturgy of the Eucharist

The liturgy of the Eucharist is the most important part of the Roman Catholic Mass — it is the point at which Catholics believe that the bread and wine are <u>transformed</u> into the body and blood of Christ. The bread and wine are usually brought in by a procession, and <u>transubstantiated</u> during a series of prayers including the <u>Institution Narrative</u> which describes Christ's words and actions during the Last Supper.

Rite of Communion

This begins with everyone saying the <u>Lord's Prayer</u>, followed by the <u>sign of peace</u>, where everyone shakes hands or hugs those around them. Following this, the congregation come forward to receive the bread and wine. Finally there is the <u>concluding rite</u>, which is a series of prayers that brings the Mass to a close. Any leftover consecrated bread and wine must be consumed by a priest, or placed in a <u>ciborium</u> (a lidded chalice) inside a 'safe' called a tabernacle.

On discovering that he had to eat the leftovers, Father Donald quickly made the switch to Communion pizza.

Non-Catholics also have a Eucharist

There are a wide variety of beliefs about the <u>importance</u> of the Eucharist, and what actually occurs during the service, for different denominations.

1) Lutherans, Methodists and most Anglicans believe that Holy Communion is more than just an '<u>intellectual</u>' commemoration of the Last Supper, it's a <u>re-enactment</u>. They believe that there is a '<u>real presence</u>' of Christ in the bread and wine. But they <u>don't</u> believe that transubstantiation occurs.

2) Reformed (Calvinist) Churches believe that the bread and wine are <u>symbolic</u> of a spiritual reality and are <u>physically unchanged</u>, but that the performance of the Eucharist does achieve '<u>spiritual nourishment</u>'.

3) Quakers and the Salvation Army don't celebrate the Eucharist or any other sacraments, seeing them as <u>unnecessary</u> or <u>inessential symbols</u> for the inward acceptance of God's grace.

Make sure you get this stuff rite...

While there are a variety of opinions as to what happens to the bread and wine during the service, Holy Communion is one of the few rites that nearly all Christian Churches have in common.

Baptism

Ritual bathing to symbolise <u>purification</u> or <u>conversion</u> was already practised by Jews before Christianity. The word 'baptism' comes from the Greek 'baptizo' meaning 'dip in water'. Not a lot of people know that.

Baptism <u>Symbolises the Washing away of <u>Sin</u></u>

1) In the Gospels, <u>John the Baptist</u> instructed people to 'repent and be baptised'. <u>Jesus</u> himself was baptised by John (Matthew 3:13-17), even though John objected to this, saying Jesus should baptise <u>him</u>.

2) After the Resurrection, Jesus told his followers to *"go and make disciples of all nations, <u>baptising</u> them in the name of the Father, and of the Son and of the Holy Spirit"* — Matthew 28:19. This is known as the 'Great Commission'.

3) Baptism symbolises a <u>new life</u> and the washing away of <u>sin</u>. A baptised person is sometimes said to be <u>born again</u>.

Roman Catholic, Orthodox and many Anglican Christians regard baptism as a <u>sacrament</u> (see page 13).

4) Christians are baptised in nearly all denominations except the <u>Salvation Army</u> and the <u>Quakers</u>.

Baptism — meant for <u>Infants</u> or <u>Believers...</u>

<u>Adults</u> can be baptised, if they haven't already been baptised as <u>babies</u>.

1) Those who regard baptism as a <u>sacrament</u> see no problem with baptising <u>infants</u>. They believe that this cleanses the baby from <u>original sin</u>, giving it a fresh start in life and making it a member of God's family.

2) Traditionally, infant baptism was especially important if the baby was <u>sick</u> and likely to die — unbaptised babies were thought to be unable to enter <u>Heaven</u>. (The Roman Catholic Church <u>doesn't</u> support this view any more, though.)

In the Early Church, it tended to be <u>adults</u> who were baptised, though whole <u>families</u> (including children) could be baptised too.

3) Baptist, Pentecostal and House Church Christians, plus those from independent fellowships, tend to receive <u>dedication</u> as <u>babies</u>, and baptism only as <u>believers</u> (called, surprisingly enough, 'believer's baptism'). They believe you shouldn't be baptised until you are old enough to decide to accept Christianity for yourself.

Baptism Services <u>can be Pretty Varied</u>

Infant Baptism

1) <u>Parents</u> and <u>godparents</u> promise to bring the child up as a part of the Christian community. They also make promises on the <u>child's behalf</u>, which will be <u>renewed</u> (if the child chooses) at <u>confirmation</u>.

2) A sign of the <u>cross</u> is made on the baby, and <u>holy water</u> is poured three times over the forehead (in the name of the Father, Son and Holy Spirit), though Orthodox Christians baptise babies by <u>total immersion</u>.

3) The baptism is conducted over a <u>font</u>, and the baby may be dressed in a <u>white robe</u> called a <u>chrisom</u> (white is the colour of <u>purity</u>).

4) A special <u>candle</u> is lit to symbolise the <u>light of Christ</u> entering the baby's life. The candle may be given to a parent or godparent to hold, to remind them of their duty to the child.

Believer's Baptism

1) This can take place in a church, a lake, a swimming pool, or even a skip. <u>Several</u> people are usually baptised at one special service.

2) Each candidate is asked <u>questions</u> about his or her faith, and may <u>explain</u> how and why he or she decided to become a Christian. He or she is then baptised by the minister by <u>total immersion</u>.

Baptism — an immersing topic...

Loads of information there — you need to know a) <u>what baptism is</u>, b) <u>why it's important</u>, c) <u>why some people do/don't agree with baptising babies</u> and d) some of the <u>common baptism rituals</u>. Get stuck in.

Features of a Christian Church

A Christian place of worship is called a <u>church</u>, <u>chapel</u> or <u>cathedral</u>. Most churches are laid out in a similar way (chapels are usually smaller and not quite so fancy, and cathedrals are really big). These pages describe typical traditional Roman Catholic and Anglican churches.

The Location of a Church is often Symbolic

1) Roman Catholic and Anglican churches are often found on the tops of <u>hills</u>. This is because they would have been the most <u>important</u> building in the area, and so needed to be easy to <u>see</u> and <u>defend</u>.

2) Churches were traditionally built from <u>local</u> stone and materials which would have been easily available. The quality of the decoration and fittings reflected the church's <u>status</u> and <u>wealth</u>.

3) They were sometimes built on ancient <u>pagan</u> sites — <u>sacred</u> groves of trees, for example. Pagans were people who worshipped a number of <u>different</u> gods, a practice much more common before Christianity became popular.

4) The <u>size</u> of the church reflected the size and wealth of the <u>parish</u>, or the wealth and status of the local <u>people</u>.

5) Seen from above, churches were often built in the shape of a <u>cross</u> aligned from east to west, so that the church faces the rising sun. This is because east is the direction of the <u>Holy Land</u>.

A Parish Church has some Typical Features

① **TOWER/SPIRE** This draws people's eyes up to Heaven, to remind them of God. It was also used in the past for <u>defence</u>, and houses the <u>church bells</u>.

② **TRANSEPTS**
The two wings of a cross-shaped church, at right angles to the nave (see page 17).

⑤ **WEATHER-VANE**
This provided a medieval public service (weather was important to farmers), and is often in the shape of a <u>cock</u> to remind people of the story of <u>St Peter</u>.

(This is usually on top of the tower.)

③ **CHURCHYARD**
This is <u>consecrated</u> ground surrounding the church, used for burials.

④ **GRAVESTONE**
A stone <u>memorial</u> marking a <u>grave</u>.

⑥ **CHURCHYARD CROSS**
The cross is the most important Christian <u>symbol</u>.

It's always crosses — why don't they build one in the shape of a fish?...

You find most parish churches that were built over a century ago look pretty similar. Chapels tend to vary more, as do more modern chapels and churches. The Roman Catholic cathedral in Liverpool is very odd, though kinda groovy (if you like that kind of thing) — but certainly not what you expect from a cathedral.

Inside a Christian Church

So that's the outside, but it's the <u>inside</u> that's more important...

Inside A Typical Parish Church

<u>Traditional</u> Roman Catholic and Anglican churches are often very similar in layout:

① ALTAR
The most important place in the church — a table which holds the items for the <u>Eucharist</u> service. The <u>altar</u> is at the east end.

③ PULPIT
A raised box from which the <u>minister</u> gives the <u>sermon</u> or talks to the congregation.

⑤ SANCTUARY
A <u>raised platform</u> where the most <u>important</u> parts of a service take place.

⑦ COVERED FONT
Used to hold <u>water</u> for <u>baptism</u>.

⑧ NAVE
The main part of the church where the <u>congregation</u> sits (or originally stood).

CONFESSIONAL BOX
A Roman Catholic Church will have a <u>partitioned compartment</u> for confession. The priest sits on one side of the partition (usually a pierced wood screen) while the confessant sits or kneels on the other side.

② EAST WINDOW
Often of <u>stained glass</u>, it's right behind the altar and draws attention to it.

④ REREDOS
Some churches have a <u>painted</u> or sculpted <u>screen</u> behind the altar. It often has pictures of Jesus, Mary or saints, and it helps to focus attention on the altar.

⑥ LECTERN
A stand for the <u>church Bible</u>. Often made from brass and in the shape of an eagle.

⑨ AISLE
Aisles are often used in <u>processions</u>.

Nonconformist Churches are a Bit Different

1) <u>Nonconformist</u> churches tend to be <u>plainly decorated</u>, with light-coloured walls and simple windows. Nonconformists believe that the traditional <u>trappings</u> of a Roman Catholic church are unnecessary, since the Bible says you can pray <u>anywhere</u> (i.e. the <u>building</u> doesn't matter). Some people feel that the simplicity of their surroundings allows them to better <u>concentrate</u> on God.

2) In <u>Roman Catholic</u>, <u>Orthodox</u> and most <u>Anglican</u> churches, the <u>focal point</u> of the building is the <u>altar</u>. This reflects the <u>liturgical</u> nature of their services and the importance of the Eucharist (see p.14). But in <u>Nonconformist</u> Churches, the focal point tends to be the <u>pulpit</u>. This is because to them, Christian <u>teaching</u>, in the form of <u>readings</u> and <u>sermons</u>, is far more important than rituals.

3) Nonconformist services tend to be <u>non-liturgical</u> (they don't use set forms or rituals). For example, some follow the '<u>hymn sandwich</u>' pattern, where hymns alternate with items like readings, prayers and a sermon. Pentecostal and House Churches may have spontaneous, often <u>charismatic</u> worship (see p.3).

4) Most Nonconformist churches don't have the cross shape that traditional Roman Catholic churches have. Nonconformist churches will tend to be more <u>square</u>, and be designed so that everyone can best <u>hear</u> what is being preached from the pulpit.

There's no sanctuary from revision...

Roman Catholic churches are filled with special objects with odd names, and it's your job to learn them all.

Christian Festivals and Holy Days

According to the Bible, no time of year is any more sacred than any other. However, certain times of year are used by Christians to commemorate, give thanks for and celebrate specific aspects of their faith.

Christian Festivals Occur Throughout the Year

ADVENT — November / December

Advent marks the start of the Christian year, and begins 4 Sundays before Christmas. It's a period of preparation for Christmas and for Christ's Second Coming. Advent candles are lit in homes and churches, and Advent calendars may be used by children to count off the days until Christmas. Orthodox Christians observe 40 days' penance (showing true sorrow for sins).

How did I get mixed up in all this?

CHRISTMAS — December 25th

Christmas celebrates the Incarnation — when God's Son came to Earth as a human being. We don't know the exact date of his birth, but we celebrate it on December 25th.

Customs vary around the world, but often date from pre-Christian times (e.g. Christmas trees). In many Roman Catholic and Anglican churches there's a 'Midnight Mass' to welcome Christmas Day, and a crib (nativity scene).

Some Christians think that the giving of expensive presents takes away the focus of what Christmas is supposed to be about. Some Protestants think that Christians should not celebrate Christmas at all, as there's no record in the Bible of the Early Church celebrating it, and it has retained too much pagan influence.

LENT — February / March

Lent commemorates the 40 days and nights of Jesus's fasting (going without food) in the wilderness after his baptism. The day before Lent is called Shrove Tuesday, a day for being 'shriven' (absolved from sin). Rich foods should be eaten up before the start of the fast and Mardi Gras carnivals may be held ('carnival' means 'farewell to meat').

On Ash Wednesday (the first day of Lent) ash is put on believers' foreheads to show that they are sorry for their sins. Few Christians today fast during Lent, but many still give up certain luxuries. Lent ends on the day before Easter.

For Roman Catholics, Lent is traditionally a sombre time where the focus of worship is on the suffering of Jesus. Catholics are obliged to abstain from meat on each Friday of Lent, and to fast (limit themselves to one main meal and two small meals a day) for a minimum of two days — Ash Wednesday and Good Friday (see below).

Some Protestant Christians do not observe Lent as it is not mentioned in the Bible, and view the practice of fasting as an attempt to achieve salvation through good works, which they believe is ineffective as salvation comes through faith alone.

HOLY WEEK — March / April

This is the final week of Lent, lasting from Palm Sunday (the Sunday before Easter, recalling Jesus's triumphal entry into Jerusalem) until the day before Easter. It commemorates Jesus's final week on Earth.

Maundy Thursday recalls the Last Supper, and Good Friday Jesus's crucifixion. There are special services, especially on Good Friday between noon and 3pm — the hours when Jesus was dying on the cross.

EASTER SUNDAY — March / April

This commemorates Jesus's resurrection. Special services are held — Roman Catholics and some Anglicans hold an Easter Vigil the night before. Easter is the most important festival of the year for most Christians, since it celebrates the victory of Jesus over death. It starts a fifty day period of focusing on the actions of the risen Christ.

Orthodox Christians keep a vigil outside their church until midnight, when the doors are flung wide and they file into a church flooded with light.

Most Protestant denominations also celebrate Easter. A very few reject it though, e.g. some Quakers (Religious Society of Friends), because they see every day as the Lord's day, with no particular day more special. Some dislike the modern use of symbols (e.g. eggs and Easter bunnies) that are believed to be associated with pre-Christian festivals.

Holy Days or holidays — who cares...

There's huge variety in the way festivals are celebrated, and many customs are cultural rather than Christian (e.g. Easter bunnies). Make sure you learn what the festivals celebrate and why, not how things are done.

Practice Questions

All this stuff should be meat and drink if you're going to get anywhere in your RS exam. Think about it... how do you expect to be able to answer an exam question about Christianity or Roman Catholicism if you don't know how people go about being Christian... So learn, learn, learn away... and then try these questions. And keep trying them until they seem as easy as eating a nice big pepperoni pizza with extra cheese and mushrooms. Mmm... pizza.

1) What is:

a) a sacrament? *(Roman Catholicism)*

b) confirmation? *(Christianity)*

c) Eucharist? *(Christianity)*

d) chrism? *(Roman Catholicism)*

e) contrition? *(Roman Catholicism)*

f) penance? *(Roman Catholicism)*

g) absolution? *(Roman Catholicism)*

h) transubstantiation?

i) Mass? *(Christianity)*

j) the penitential rite? *(Roman Catholicism)*

k) the liturgy of the word? *(Roman Catholicism)*

l) the liturgy of the Eucharist? *(Roman Catholicism)*

m) the rite of communion? *(Roman Catholicism)*

n) real presence (in the Eucharist)? *(Christianity)*

o) believer's baptism? *(Christianity)*

p) non-liturgical worship? *(Christianity)*

q) charismatic worship? *(Christianity)*

r) Advent? *(Christianity)*

s) Lent? *(Christianity)*

t) Holy Week?

These are for 2 marks each. There are a lot of terms here, so make doubly sure you learn all the key words for your Unit. It'll help with the other questions as well.

2) For each of the following questions, give <u>two</u> reasons for your point of view.

a) Do you think it's important for a Christian/Roman Catholic to be confirmed?

b) Do you think that the Eucharist is the most important sacrament? *(Roman Catholicism)*

c) Do you think infants should be baptised?

d) Do you think Christians/Roman Catholics should celebrate Christmas?

4 marks — but to get them you need to give <u>two</u> reasons

3) For these questions, take extra care with your spelling, punctuation and grammar, and express yourself as clearly as possible.

a) Explain why the sacrament of reconciliation is important to Roman Catholics. *(Roman Catholicism)*

b) Explain why the different elements of the Mass are important to Roman Catholics. *(Roman Catholicism)*

c) Explain the importance of baptism to Christians/Roman Catholics.

d) Explain the differences between a typical Roman Catholic church and a typical Nonconformist church. *(Christianity)*

e) Explain why many Christians/Roman Catholics think that Easter is the most important event in the Christian calendar.

You can take a little bit more time to set out what you know with these — they're worth an astonishing 8 marks

4) Read the following statements:

a) "The seven sacraments are all vehicles for God's grace."

b) "A child should be baptised as soon as possible."

c) "It shouldn't matter to a Christian what their church looks like."

d) "All Christians should give something up for Lent."

For each statement:

(i) Do you agree? Give reasons for your opinion.

(ii) Give reasons why some people may disagree with you.

In your answers you should refer to Christianity/Roman Catholic Christianity.

These are the questions where you can show you've learned what different people think. They're worth 6 marks.

Vocation

Some people experience a specific <u>call</u> from God to lead a <u>Christian life</u>. This calling is known as a <u>vocation</u>.

You can *Respond to God* Through a *Vocation*

1) Some people feel that they've experienced a <u>call</u> from God to lead a <u>Christian life</u>. This 'calling' is known as a <u>vocation</u>.

2) It can be a job, but isn't always. Many Christians who feel they have a vocation believe God has created them with the right <u>talents</u> for their mission.

3) Christians believe they <u>know</u> if something's their vocation — they feel <u>drawn to it</u>, and '<u>at home</u>' when they're doing it. But vocations are often <u>challenging</u>. Christians believe you need <u>God's help</u> to do them.

4) There are <u>lots</u> of different vocations a Christian might be called to. Here are a few examples:

- joining a religious community as a <u>monk</u> or a <u>nun</u> (see below).
- taking <u>holy orders</u> (being <u>ordained</u>) to become a <u>deacon</u>, <u>priest</u> or <u>bishop</u> (see p.11). A deacon is one step below a priest in the Church <u>hierarchy</u>. A Roman Catholic deacon may carry out any of the duties of a priest, apart from celebrating Mass (see p.14), hearing confession or anointing the sick (see p.13). <u>Married men</u> can become Roman Catholic deacons, but not priests.
- carrying out <u>missionary work</u> — trying to convert people to Christianity.
- training for a non-religious job such as <u>medicine</u>, <u>teaching</u> or <u>social work</u>.
- <u>volunteering</u> in the <u>community</u> — e.g. running a youth group.
- <u>charity work</u> — either religion-based (e.g. Christian Aid), or secular (e.g. Greenpeace).
- <u>marriage</u> and <u>raising children</u>.

5) You have to actually <u>choose</u> to follow your vocation — it doesn't just <u>happen</u>.

Monks *and* Nuns *are Members of* Religious Orders

1) Those who become <u>monks</u> or <u>nuns</u> take vows of:

POVERTY, *CHASTITY* and *OBEDIENCE*

These three rules are known as the <u>evangelical counsels</u>. They're generally believed to be only for those with this specific religious <u>calling</u>.

2) Some religious orders stress <u>service</u> to the poor, sick or destitute. Members of orders that go out into society are said to live the <u>active life</u>.

3) Others go in for <u>prayer</u> and <u>study</u> — the <u>contemplative life</u>. Contemplative orders are usually 'enclosed' <u>religious communities</u>, where members live together and rarely (if ever) leave their monasteries.

4) Someone who lives as a monk or nun in a religious community is said to live a <u>monastic life</u>.

There's loads more about <u>religious communities</u> *on page 5.*

Mother Teresa's 'Missionaries of Charity', and the 'Franciscans' are examples of those living the <u>active life</u>.

'The Carmelites' and 'Poor Clares' (for women), and the 'Carthusians' or 'Cistercians' (for men) live the <u>contemplative life</u>.

Some Christians Work Toward *Community Cohesion*

1) Some Christians feel a vocation to <u>help their community</u>, and to try to bring it <u>together</u>. Different groups sharing a common <u>vision</u> of the community, and feeling a <u>part</u> of it, is known as <u>community cohesion</u>.

2) One organisation that works to encourage community cohesion in the north-west of England is the <u>Bolton Christian Community Cohesion Project</u>. They organise events to get the whole of the community together, regardless of faith, creating a way for different faith groups to get know each other. They encourage Christian groups to try to serve all of Bolton's ethnic and religious communities.

Religious orders — learn all this stuff really well...

Most Christians believe that they should seek to discover what God is <u>calling</u> them to do. There are some examples above, but there are millions of others. And when it comes to writing about vocation in daily life and work, it's probably best to choose something that <u>you</u> have an interest in.

Christian Values

Jesus was a Jew, so his values were grounded in <u>Jewish</u> belief — the laws found in the <u>Old Testament</u>.

The <u>Ten Commandments</u> — show some <u>Respect</u>

The most famous laws in the Old Testament are the <u>Ten Commandments</u> given to Moses in Exodus 20. Different Christian traditions number the commandments in different ways. Here's the Roman Catholic/Lutheran list:

1) You shall have <u>no other gods before me</u>.
You shall not make for yourself an <u>idol</u>.
2) You shall not <u>misuse the name of the Lord</u>.
3) Observe the <u>Sabbath</u> and keep it holy.
4) Honour your <u>father and mother</u>.
5) You shall not <u>kill</u>.

6) You shall not commit <u>adultery</u>.
7) You shall not <u>steal</u>.
8) You shall not <u>give false testimony</u> (lie).
9) You shall not <u>covet</u> your neighbour's wife.
10) You shall not <u>covet</u> your neighbour's goods.*

* To <u>covet</u> is to desperately want something (that you're not allowed to have).

Look at my lovely tablets.

Most Christians believe that it's <u>necessary</u> to try to stick to the Ten Commandments.
The <u>Roman Catholic Church</u> teaches that observance of them is necessary for <u>salvation</u>.

The Commandments are about <u>Respecting God...</u>

The <u>first three</u> commandments are about showing <u>respect to God</u>.

1) The first calls for <u>monotheism</u>. Worshippers of God mustn't worship <u>anything else</u> — including <u>idols</u>.
2) The second commandment demands respect for the <u>name</u> of the Lord. Not only does this ban using "God" or "Jesus" as <u>swear words</u>, but also using God's name to back up a <u>lie</u> or in a <u>dishonest manner</u>.
3) Different Christian groups place greater or less emphasis on the third commandment of observing the <u>Sabbath</u>. This is God's instruction to take <u>one day</u> out of the week and keep it <u>holy</u>. Traditionally, the Sabbath was a day dedicated to God and family on which <u>no work</u> was allowed to be done.
4) For most Christians, the Sabbath day is <u>Sunday</u> — the Lord's Day — as this was the day of Christ's resurrection (although <u>Seventh-day Adventists</u>, keep their Sabbath on Saturdays, like the Jews).
5) In the UK, laws against working on a Sunday have gradually been relaxed as society has become less religious. An organisation called <u>Keep Sunday Special</u> campaigns for stricter rules on Sunday trading — both to help religious people keep the Sabbath, and to secure a day that families can spend together.

...and <u>Other People</u>

The <u>last seven</u> commandments are about showing respect for <u>other people</u>.

1) Some Christians believe that the fourth commandment, which calls for the <u>honouring of your father and mother</u>, includes respect not only for extended family members but also to those placed in positions of <u>responsibility</u> and authority, such as teachers.
2) The fifth commandment, <u>not to kill</u>, is interpreted in different ways. Most Churches are willing to make exceptions for killing in <u>war</u> — but some groups, like the Religious Society of Friends (Quakers), are <u>pacifists</u> and are against fighting and killing under any circumstances.
3) Many Christian Churches take the commandment not to kill as a ban on <u>abortion</u>.
4) Many modern Bibles translate the commandment as *"You shall not <u>murder</u>"*, which allows for killing in <u>war</u> and <u>capital punishment</u>. They argue this interpretation is more in keeping with the rest of the Old Testament.
5) The sixth, seventh and eighth commandments ban <u>adultery</u> (cheating on your partner), <u>theft</u> and <u>lying</u>.
6) The last two are perhaps the <u>subtlest</u> of the commandments. You don't have to actually <u>do</u> anything to break them — you break them just by <u>lusting</u> after a married woman (or man), or <u>yearning</u> for something that belongs to someone else. These commandments are closely linked to the sin of <u>envy</u>.

Number 11 — You shall learn this page...

It's always a good idea to know the rules — that way you won't break them accidentally. But if in doubt, 'respect' is a good place to start. If something feels disrespectful, you probably shouldn't be doing it.

The Sermon on the Mount

The Sermon on the Mount is a summary of Jesus's teachings on how Christians are supposed to live.

The Sermon on the Mount — the Christian Ideal

The Sermon on the Mount is one of the most important summaries of Jesus's moral teaching found in the Gospels. It appears as a collection in Matthew 5:1-7:29, but much of the same material is also in Luke. Some say that the Sermon on the Mount preaches an ideal, which no one can live up to. But others argue that Christians can still aspire to this ideal, though no one can be totally perfect (this side of the grave, anyway).

Jesus Reinterprets the Law of Moses (Matthew 5:17-48)

1) In the Sermon, Jesus reinterprets the Law of Moses — the rules given by God in the Old Testament.

2) Jesus takes these laws and makes them more strict and more internal. Where the Law of Moses calls for people not to kill, Jesus orders us to go further and not be angry with each other. Where the Law of Moses orders us not to commit adultery, Jesus warns that looking upon someone lustfully is sinful in itself. Jesus takes commandments about actions and makes them about intentions and emotions.

3) Jesus speaks about anger, adultery, divorce, vows, revenge and love for our enemies: "*If someone strikes you on the right cheek, turn to him the other also.*"

Displaying Religion (Matthew 6:1-18)

1) Jesus orders his followers to do their praying, giving to charity, and fasting quietly and without trying to impress other people.

2) Jesus says that those who do good things in secret will be rewarded by God. But that those who deliberately do good work in front of a crowd, known as 'displaying religion', have already had their reward in the effect it has on their audience.

3) Jesus calls those who display religion hypocrites — people who act out beliefs they don't really hold, or whose actions don't match what they say.

4) Most modern Christians take this to mean that, while prayers, charity and fasting don't need to be done in private, they should be done for God alone, with no thought of trying to impress others.

> It's in this part of the Gospel that Jesus teaches his followers the Lord's Prayer — "*Our Father in heaven, hallowed be your name...*"

Christians and Money (Matthew 6:19-34)

1) Jesus orders his followers not to seek material riches ("*treasures on earth*"), or even material security, but rather spiritual riches ("*treasures in heaven*"). He says "*You cannot serve both God and Money.*"

2) He tells his followers that it's wrong to even worry about material things : "*Look at the birds of the air; they do not sow or reap or store away in barns, and yet your heavenly Father feeds them. Are you not much more valuable than they? Who of you by worrying can add a single hour to his life?*"

3) Most Christians don't take these verses to mean that we shouldn't save money, but rather that our main concern should be with spiritual things and helping other people.

Christians and Judgement and The Golden Rule (Matthew 7:1-12)

1) Jesus warns his followers "*Do not judge, or you too will be judged.*" He uses the image of someone trying to remove a speck of sawdust from another man's eye when they have a plank in their own.

2) Most Christians interpret this as meaning they should strictly judge their own moral state before looking at other people's, and that they must be charitable and forgiving of other people's failings.

And another thing...

3) Jesus then states what's known as the Golden Rule:

> "*do to others what you would have them do to you, for this sums up the Law and the Prophets.*"

Many Christians use the Golden Rule as moral rule of thumb.

Don't pass judgement on others — that's the examiner's job...

The Bible's a long book (you've probably noticed) — but Matthew 5, 6 and 7 give you the gist of Jesus's teachings.

Section Four — Living the Christian Life

Christian Charities in the UK

Christians, like all people with a religious faith, try to act in a way that's consistent with their beliefs. For many this means getting involved in charity — giving time and money to help people in need.

Christians have a Duty to Relieve Poverty

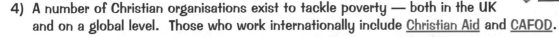

"Rich nations have a grave moral responsibility towards those which are unable to ensure the means of their development by themselves..." from the Catechism of the Roman Catholic Church

1) All Christian denominations have become more concerned with a fairer distribution of wealth. A key question is whether wealth ultimately belongs to God, and should therefore be for the good of everyone.

2) Charity is an important part of Christianity, and a concern for Christians is whether or not they should be wealthy. Jesus spoke of giving up wealth to help the poor.

"...the love of money is a root of all kinds of evil." 1 Timothy 6:10

3) Jesus also said that we have an obligation to love each other, and that if we help those who need it, it is as if we are helping Jesus himself (see p.4).

4) A number of Christian organisations exist to tackle poverty — both in the UK and on a global level. Those who work internationally include Christian Aid and CAFOD.

The Passage helps the Homeless in London

1) The Passage is a Roman Catholic organisation that was started in 1980 by the Daughters of Charity of St Vincent de Paul and Westminster Cathedral to help the homeless.

2) The Passage runs a hostel (i.e. temporary accommodation) in London for homeless people, with priority given to the most vulnerable.

3) Although The Passage does provide a Roman Catholic chaplaincy service if requested, it doesn't carry out any deliberate evangelical work.

4) It also offers medical care, skills training and advice to help homeless people get jobs and build new lives for themselves.

The Salvation Army is a Church and a Registered Charity

1) The Salvation Army was founded in London in 1878. It's a Protestant Church and a charity that works to help the poor and homeless in the UK and across the world.

2) The Salvation Army runs a number of hostels, which give homeless people a safe, clean place to live that's off the streets. They try to help those who come to their hostels get back into employment and independent living. The Salvation Army also helps unite families who have lost contact, and runs services to help those with drink and drug problems.

3) A substantial amount of the funding for The Salvation Army's work comes from running charity shops up and down the UK.

Church Action on Poverty Campaigns for the Poor

1) Church Action on Poverty is a national ecumenical (i.e. made up of different denominations) charity that works to reduce poverty in the UK. They encourage churches to get active in helping the poor.

2) They campaign on a number of issues, such as securing rights for asylum seekers and trying to get a raise in the minimum wage. They also try to help people in poverty have an influence on the decisions that affect them, e.g. decisions made by local government.

"Let us not love with words... but with actions and in truth..."

(1 John 3:18) This page is one of the best adverts for Christianity. Regardless of your religious beliefs, it's difficult to argue with any group that gets out into the world and actually spends its time helping people. As Jesus says, "a tree is recognised by its fruit" — and there's some pretty good fruit right here.

Practice Questions

There are many different ways that Christians can express their sense of vocation — as a priest or a monk or a nun, or by talking to other people about their faith, or by dedicating their lives to helping people. For now however, your exam is 'calling' you to get this stuff learnt — and to help you along that road, here are some revision questions for you to have a crack at. Remember, you need to keep trying them till you can do them all without any help.

1) **What is/are:**

   a) vocation?

   b) holy orders?

   c) a religious community?

   d) the monastic life?

   e) the active life?

   f) the contemplative life?

   g) the evangelical counsels?

   h) the Sermon on the Mount?

   i) the Law of Moses?

   j) displaying religion?

   k) a hypocrite?

   l) charity?

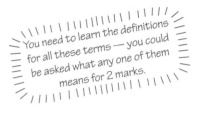

You need to learn the definitions for all these terms — you could be asked what any one of them means for 2 marks.

2) **For each of the following questions, give <u>two</u> reasons for your point of view.**

   a) Do you think that being Christian should affect how people live their lives?

   b) Do you think that people should follow the Ten Commandments?

   c) Do you think it is possible for someone to follow all the teachings in the Sermon on the Mount?

   d) Do you think that charity is the most important element of the Christian life?

4 marks for these. Make sure you get two good reasons down, and then move on.

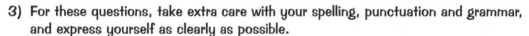

3) **For these questions, take extra care with your spelling, punctuation and grammar, and express yourself as clearly as possible.**

   a) Explain how some Christians fulfil their vocation in a religious order.

   b) Explain how some Christians use the Ten Commandments as a guide to living.

   c) Explain how Jesus reinterprets the Law of Moses in the Sermon on the Mount.

   d) Explain how one Christian/Roman Catholic organisation helps relieve poverty and suffering in the UK.

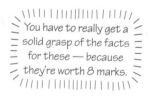

You have to really get a solid grasp of the facts for these — because they're worth 8 marks.

4) **Read the following statements:**

   a) "You can serve God better in an active life than in a contemplative life."

   b) "All Ten Commandments are equally important."

   c) "Christians should only pray in private."

   d) "For Christians, helping those in need should be more important than evangelising."

   For each statement:

   (i) Do you agree? Give reasons for your opinion.

   (ii) Give reasons why some people may disagree with you.

   In your answers you should refer to Christianity/Roman Catholic Christianity.

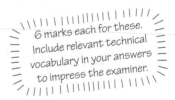

6 marks each for these. Include relevant technical vocabulary in your answers to impress the examiner.

The Nature of Discipleship

Christianity sees Jesus as the <u>Son of God</u> — and so his story is pretty important.

The Gospels — Good News, but Not Biographies

1) The <u>Gospels</u> were written to <u>preserve</u> the story of Jesus after the apostles died.

2) They also pointed to the coming of the '<u>kingdom of God</u>'.
The 'kingdom of God' is the <u>rulership</u> of God in people's lives.
In the Gospels, it either refers to the <u>total acceptance</u> of God in someone's heart, or to the <u>final</u> Kingdom after Judgement Day.

> Jesus went into Galilee, proclaiming... 'The kingdom of God is near. Repent and believe the good news!' Mark 1:14-15

3) An early Christian wrote that Mark was the 'interpreter of Peter', but that he hadn't known Jesus <u>personally</u>. Mark may have used early <u>collections</u> of Jesus's words and actions, or he may have got information from <u>Peter</u> (see pages 27 and 33 for more about Peter.).

The Calling of the Disciples — Jesus Gathered Followers

1) The word '<u>disciple</u>' means '<u>follower</u>', and is often used to refer to one of Jesus's followers from the Gospels. But it can also be used more generally to mean <u>any</u> Christian.

> Follow me!

2) Mark tells us that Jesus called as his first disciples: <u>Simon</u>, <u>Andrew</u>, <u>John</u>, <u>James</u> and <u>Levi</u>.

The Calling of the First Disciples (Mark 1:14-20)
As Jesus walked by the Sea of Galilee, he came across four fishermen: Simon (who he later called Peter or 'rock'), Andrew, and the 'sons of Zebedee' — James and John.

> "'Come, follow me,' Jesus said, 'and I will make you fishers of men.'"

They all abandoned their nets and followed Jesus.

The Calling of Levi (Mark 2:13-17)
Jesus called a tax collector, Levi, to follow him. He had dinner with Levi and other people the Pharisees called 'sinners':

> "...they asked his disciples: 'Why does he eat with tax collectors and 'sinners'?' On hearing this, Jesus said to them, 'It is not the healthy who need a doctor, but the sick. I have not come to call the righteous, but sinners.'"

3) Jesus <u>didn't</u> choose to call well-educated, religious men, e.g. the Sadducees (Jewish priests) or Pharisees (teachers of the Law). Instead he called <u>common fishermen</u> to learn from him and serve God.

4) He also called Levi to be a disciple — a <u>tax collector</u>. Tax collectors were <u>strongly disliked</u> by most Jews, because they worked for the occupying Romans. (According to the Gospel of Matthew, Levi is Matthew the Apostle.)

5) Most modern Christians believe these two passages show that <u>anyone</u> can be a follower of Jesus. It doesn't matter what your <u>background</u> is, or how much you've <u>sinned</u> in the past. Anyone who repents and <u>follows</u> Jesus is welcome.

The Mission of the Disciples — Go Out and Preach

1) Over time, Jesus called other disciples to him until he had '<u>the Twelve</u>' (later known as the <u>apostles</u>).

2) He sent the disciples out <u>in pairs</u> to tell the people of Israel the <u>good news</u> of the <u>kingdom of God</u>.

The Sending Out of the Twelve (Mark 6:7-13)
Jesus sent his disciples out with authority over evil spirits. They were to take a staff — but should not take bread, money, a bag or an extra coat. Where they were made welcome, they were to stay in that place until they left town. Where they were not made welcome, they were to shake the dust from their feet as a marker to others.

> "They went out and preached that people should repent. They drove out many demons and anointed many sick people with oil and healed them." Mark 6:12-13

3) The disciples were told to <u>trust in God</u> and He would provide for them during their <u>mission</u> (through the charity of others). Many Christians believe that they should be prepared to do the same.

4) This passage also carries a message to Christians today about <u>giving charity</u>. They should be among the people who would welcome the apostles, rather than those who turn them away.

This stuff is true — it's all gospel, mate...

'Following' Jesus was a bit more literal back then — the disciples travelled together with Jesus as he preached.

The Costs of Discipleship

Jesus Said there were Costs of Being a Disciple

True Family   ...a disciple's true family is his fellow believers.

> "Then Jesus' mother and brothers arrived. Standing outside, they sent someone in to call him... 'Who are my mother and my brothers?' [Jesus] asked. Then he looked at those seated in a circle around him and said, 'Here are my mother and my brothers! Whoever does God's will is my brother and sister and mother.'" Mark 3:31-35

1) Some Christians interpret this as Jesus rejecting his physical family in favour of his 'spiritual' family — that he was telling his disciples to forget blood ties and find a new family in God.

2) Many modern Christians are uncomfortable with these ideas, and feel that you should love and respect your family whatever their beliefs

3) Others interpret the 'true family' teachings as expanding, not replacing, a Christian's family. In following Jesus, you become part of a worldwide family of believers.

True Greatness   ...a disciple must be the servant of all.

1) In Mark 9:33-37, the disciples argue on the road through Galilee to Capernaum about who among them is the greatest.

2) They tried to hide their argument from Jesus, but he responded by saying that true greatness comes through serving others:

> "If anyone wants to be first, he must be the very last, and the servant of all.'" Mark 9:35

3) Putting yourself last like this involves a great deal of self-sacrifice (putting other people's needs before your own). Although most Christians see this as an ideal, it can be a very hard teaching to follow.

The Rich Man   ...a disciple must follow the commandments faithfully and give all he has to the poor.

1) In Mark 10:17-31, a wealthy man asks Jesus, "what must I do to inherit eternal life?"

2) Jesus said he must do two things: follow the commandments (the ten laws in Exodus 20) and give his wealth to the poor.

> "...sell everything you have and give to the poor, and you will have treasure in heaven.'" Mark 10:21

> "How hard it is for the rich to enter the kingdom of God!... It is easier for a camel to go through the eye of a needle than for a rich man to enter the kingdom of God.'" Mark 10:23-25

3) He told his disciples that it was desperately hard for a rich person to enter the kingdom of God, although everything is possible for God.

4) He went on to tell the disciples that whatever they gave up now, they'd get a hundred times as much, both now and in the future, i.e. you may face hardship now, but there's eternal life in the end.

5) This story causes big problems for some modern Christians. If a person sells everything they have, they're left with no way of looking after themselves — and so become a burden on other people. And how rich is too rich? In the developed world, are we all too rich to enter the kingdom of God? Also, many modern Christians fail to keep all the commandments (e.g. most Christians do work of some sort (gardening, cleaning, paying bills, etc.) on Sunday, the Christian Sabbath — "Remember the Sabbath day by keeping it holy... On it you shall not do any work..." Exodus 20:8-10)

The Parable of the Tenants   ...discipleship is dangerous.

1) In Mark 12:1-12, Jesus tells a parable about the dangers and responsibilities faced by God's servants:

A man left his vineyard in the hands of tenants. He sent servants to collect the rent that was due — but all were beaten or killed by the tenants. In the end he sent his own son, but the tenants killed him too so that the vineyard would become theirs. The owner responded by killing the tenants and giving the vineyard to others.

2) This parable is told to the chief priests and the Pharisees — they are compared to the tenants who would kill the son (Jesus) for their own ends. The vineyard owner represents God.

3) This parable also warned the disciples that they risked persecution and death for carrying God's message. The same warning applies to some Christians today — in some parts of the world, people are still discriminated against, beaten or even killed for their faith.

No one ever said it was gonna be easy...

Jesus expected his disciples to give up everything and risk their lives to be servants of God and men. Hard.

The Problems of Discipleship

Jesus's disciples were only human. They didn't always <u>understand</u>, and sometimes they <u>failed</u>.

The Disciples Couldn't Cast a Spirit from a Boy

1) When the disciples were sent out to preach in Mark 6 (see p.25), Jesus gave them <u>authority</u> over evil spirits. They were <u>expected</u> to heal and perform exorcisms in Jesus's name, just as Jesus did himself.

> ### The Boy with an Evil Spirit (Mark 9:14-29)
> The disciples attempted to cure a boy with an evil spirit but failed. When Jesus arrived, he called the people an *"unbelieving generation"*, and told the father that the boy could only be healed if he showed faith. The father replied that he believed, but needed help to have enough faith. Jesus cast the spirit out, and told his disciples that the demon could *"come out only by prayer"*.

> *"...the boy's father exclaimed, 'I do believe; help me overcome my unbelief!'"* Mark 9:24

2) So according to Mark, the disciples failed because the <u>people</u> didn't have <u>faith</u>, and hadn't been <u>praying</u> for the miracle. Jesus was able to drive out the demon because the father <u>exercised</u> what little faith he had.

The Sower — Should Only Some People Get It?

> Well don't ask me.

1) According to Mark 4:1-20, Jesus told a story about a <u>farmer</u> sowing seed:

> ### The Parable of the Sower (Mark 4:1-20)
> A farmer scattered seeds across the ground. Some fell on the path and were eaten by birds. Some fell in shallow soil, and grew up quickly, but died because the plants had no roots. Some fell among thorns and the plants were choked. But some fell on good soil and *"produced a crop, multiplying thirty, sixty, or even a hundred times"*.

2) This is a rare example of Jesus using <u>allegory</u> in his parables — the story is <u>entirely symbolic</u>, with the seeds and the soils representing the <u>word of God</u> and the <u>hearers of the Gospel</u> respectively.

3) Mark says that Jesus followed the parable with the call, *"He who has ears to hear, let him hear"*, and then delivered one of the most <u>controversial</u> passages in the Gospels to the disciples (Mark 4:10-12):
   • He said that he spoke in parables so that the crowds <u>wouldn't understand him</u>.
   • He didn't <u>want</u> the crowds to understand, because *"otherwise they might turn and be <u>forgiven</u>!"*

4) Jesus was <u>disappointed</u> with his disciples, because they needed him to explain the parable — they had <u>failed</u> to understand. But Jesus went on to explain it to them, and <u>only</u> to them (Mark 4:13-20).

More Failures: Rivalry, Gethsemane, Peter's Denial

It <u>wasn't easy</u> being a disciple of Jesus. Mark highlights, in particular, the failings of those <u>closest</u> to Jesus — James and John (the sons of Zebedee) and Simon Peter.

> ### Rivalry and Service (Mark 10:41-45)
> James and John asked Jesus to let them sit at his right and left hands in heaven. Jesus told all the disciples that they shouldn't want to *"lord it"* over other people, and repeated what he'd said earlier about true greatness (see p.26): *"...whoever wants to become great among you must be your servant, and whoever wants to be first must be slave of all. For even the Son of Man did not come to be served, but to serve..."*

> ### Prayers at Gethsemane (Mark 14:27-42)
> Jesus told the disciples that they would all abandon him, and he predicted Peter's denial. All the disciples swore they'd never disown him.
> Jesus then took Peter, James and John to keep guard while he prayed in the garden of Gethsemane. Three times he went to pray for an hour. Each time, when he returned, he found all three disciples asleep.

> ### Peter's Denial (Mark 14:66-72)
> After Jesus was arrested, Peter was asked three times if he was with Jesus. Three times, he denied it: *"He began to call down curses on himself, and he swore to them, 'I don't know this man you're talking about.'"* — then he broke down in tears when he realised that Jesus had been right.

These stories cause <u>problems</u> for some modern Christians. If the <u>disciples</u> (even <u>Peter</u>, the first Bishop of Rome) couldn't obey Jesus, and repeatedly <u>failed</u> him, what chance do they have?

On the other hand, the <u>humanity</u> of the disciples can help Christians to cope with their <u>own</u> failings. Jesus loved his disciples despite their shortcomings — he didn't expect perfection from them, just as he doesn't expect it from us.

Discipleship — is that the one that Jesus walked on water to...

Reading Mark, it's easy to see Peter as a failure. He questioned Jesus, didn't seem to understand a lot of the time, fell asleep at Gethsemane, ran away when Jesus was arrested and denied knowing him three times. But it was Peter who first recognised Jesus as the Christ, and who led the Church following the resurrection.

Jesus in Conflict with Jewish Law

There's evidence of <u>conflict</u> all through Mark's Gospel. And some of the most <u>memorable</u> parts of the Gospel are where Jesus argues about the Law (the laws handed down by God in the Torah) with the <u>Pharisees</u>.

The Pharisees and Scribes were Experts in the Law

1) The <u>Pharisees</u> were a Jewish sect who <u>studied</u> the Law of Moses, and were dedicated to keeping the Jewish faith alive. They believed that obedience to the <u>Law</u> was all important.
2) The <u>scribes</u> were <u>religious lawyers</u>. They made copies of the Torah, and so knew the Law very well.
3) Jesus was often in <u>conflict</u> with the Pharisees and scribes for breaking laws or traditions. For example, Jesus dined with <u>sinners</u> (Mark 2:13-17) and his disciples didn't <u>fast</u> (go without food as sign of devotion to God) (Mark 2:18-20). Jesus explained that his followers would only fast once he was dead.

Jesus Forgave and Healed a Paralysed Man

The Paralysed Man (Mark 2:1-12)
A paralysed man was brought to Jesus. Jesus saw the faith in the man and those who had brought him, and forgave the man for his sins. Some teachers of the Law (scribes) thought this was blasphemy, since they believed only God could forgive sins. Jesus asked whether it was easier to forgive sins or cure a paralysed man. The man then got up and walked, proving that *"the Son of Man has authority on earth to forgive sins"*.

"Which is easier: to say to the paralytic, 'Your sins are forgiven,' or to say, 'Get up, take your mat and walk'?" Mark 2:9

He said People were More Important than the Sabbath...

The <u>Sabbath</u> (Saturday) is the Jewish day of rest, when Jews aren't supposed to do any <u>work</u>.

Picking Grain on the Sabbath (Mark 2:23-28)
The Pharisees accused the disciples of working on the Sabbath when they picked grain. Jesus reminded them that even King David broke the Law when he was hungry and in need, by eating bread meant only for priests. He said *"the Sabbath was made for man, not man for the Sabbath"*.

The Man with the Shrivelled Hand (Mark 3:1-6)
Jesus cured a man with a shrivelled hand in a synagogue on the Sabbath — the Pharisees saw this healing as work, and so forbidden. Jesus asked, *"Which is lawful on the Sabbath: to do good or to do evil, to save life or to kill?"* The Pharisees' stubbornness distressed Jesus.

In both cases, Jesus <u>justified</u> working on the Sabbath on the grounds that <u>human need</u> should come before religious laws, and that preventing or repairing harm is <u>always</u> a good thing.

...and Challenged Traditions

Mark tells us that Jesus challenged the traditions of <u>ritual cleanliness</u> (laws on food and washing that prevented anything 'unclean' entering a Jew's body) and <u>corban</u> (a gift dedicated to God).

Ritual Cleanliness (Mark 7:1-8 and 7:14-23)
The Pharisees had elaborate laws about washing before eating in order to stay ritually clean. Jesus argued that it's not what goes into a man that makes him unclean, but rather, what comes out of him.

"What comes out of a man is what makes him 'unclean'. For from within, out of men's hearts, come evil thoughts, sexual immorality, theft, murder, adultery, greed, malice, deceit, lewdness, envy, slander, arrogance and folly." Mark 7:20-22

These views would have caused <u>major conflict</u> within the Jewish community at the time.

But many Christians believe that putting people's <u>welfare</u> before strict religious rules, and always trying to be a <u>good person</u>, should be the basis for good <u>community cohesion</u>.

Corban (Mark 7:9-13)
Jesus argued that the Jews were more concerned with their own traditions than God's word. The example he gave was that of corban. The priests allowed people to leave their parents destitute, which goes against God's Law, if they were giving everything to the Temple as a gift to God (corban).

Those pesky Pharisees — they just kept turning up...
There isn't room here to put in the full texts from the Gospel, so make sure you go away and read all the relevant bits for yourself. <u>Learning</u> a few of those quotes wouldn't go amiss come exam time, either.

Jesus in Conflict with Authority

It wasn't just lawyers that Jesus fought with — he doesn't seem to have been a fan of authority in general.

The Sadducees were a Group of Priests

1) The Sadducees were a group of priests who ran the Temple in Jerusalem (the building where burnt sacrifices were made to God). They believed in sticking very rigidly to the books of the Torah, and they didn't believe in the resurrection of the dead.

2) The chief priests feared Jesus and wanted him dead.

Jesus Sparked Conflict when he Entered Jerusalem

The Triumphal Entry (Mark 11:1-11)
When Jesus entered Jerusalem at the end of his journeys around Israel, he entered as a King. He was carried on the back of a colt (a young horse) while the people cried: *"Hosanna!"* and *"Blessed is the coming kingdom of our father David!"*. Cloaks and palm branches were spread along the road for his horse to walk on.

This is the event that Christians celebrate on Palm Sunday, the Sunday before Good Friday.

The Cleansing of the Temple (Mark 11:15-18)
In the Temple courtyard in Jerusalem, Jesus found a market, with *"money changers"* and *"those selling doves"*. He overturned their tables and drove the traders out, saying they'd turned the Temple into *"a den of robbers"*.

The Authority of Jesus Questioned (Mark 11:27-33)
The chief priests and elders asked Jesus on who's authority he was acting. He replied with a question about John the Baptist: *"Answer me, and I will tell you by what authority... John's baptism — was it from heaven, or from men?"* Saying *"from heaven"* meant admitting they were wrong about John, but saying *"from men"* would anger the people (who believed John was a prophet). So they couldn't answer.

1) In each of these examples, the conflict is about authority. Jesus is implying that his authority is greater than the priests in the Temple, because he's acting for God — but he never actually says that.

2) Instead, he quotes scripture as he clears the Temple (in Mark 11:17 he quotes Isaiah and Jeremiah) and traps his opponents with an unanswerable question.

Jesus Argued about Resurrection and Taxes

Marriage at the Resurrection (Mark 12:18-27)
The Sadducees didn't believe in resurrection of the dead, and they tried to catch Jesus out with an awkward question. The Jews had a custom called levirate marriage, where if a man died childless, his brother must marry his widow. The Sadducees imagined a woman who married seven brothers in turn in this way. They asked Jesus: *"At the resurrection whose wife will she be, since the seven were married to her?"* Jesus replied that after the resurrection, people would be *"like the angels in heaven"*, and so wouldn't be married at all. In favour of resurrection, Jesus argued: *"He is not the God of the dead, but of the living."*

1) This story is quite significant for modern Christians. It shows that the idea of resurrection was around before Jesus, challenging the belief that life after death depends on a belief in Jesus Christ.

2) It describes life after the resurrection as very different from life on earth.

3) Also, the statement that God is God *"of the living"* implies that judgement and resurrection come at death, rather than people staying dead until the Last Day.

4) Another time, the authorities tried to catch Jesus out with a question about taxes to Rome:

5) This passage has been used to justify various different positions over the years, e.g., that Church and State should be separate, that Christians are obliged to obey State laws, or that money is an earthly thing that distracts you from God.

Paying Taxes (Mark 12:13-17)
Jesus avoided the trap of some Pharisees and Herod's men when they asked him whether it was right to pay taxes to Caesar. He asked them to bring him a coin and tell him whose picture was on it: *"'Caesar's,' they replied. Then Jesus said to them, 'Give to Caesar what is Caesar's and to God what is God's.'"*

The two things you can be certain of — death and taxes...

Jesus was prepared to challenge authority when he felt it was necessary, but he was no anarchist. He didn't condone not paying taxes, and most of his anger was directed at what he saw as hypocrisy and impiety.

Jesus in Conflict with His Followers

Mark doesn't record <u>many</u> arguments between Jesus and his followers, but there were a few.

Jesus Predicted his Passion Three Times

1) The '<u>Passion</u>' was the <u>suffering</u> of Jesus in the time leading up to his <u>death</u>.
2) He <u>predicted</u> his passion, and according to Mark, he told his disciples about it <u>three times</u>.

> *Jesus's Prediction of the Passion* (Mark 8:31-33)
> Jesus taught his disciples that he must suffer and die, but would be resurrected on the third day:
> Peter took Jesus to one side *"and began to rebuke him"* (by telling Jesus it would never happen to him — Mark isn't specific, but Matthew 16:22 is).
> Jesus reacted angrily to Peter: *"'Get behind me, Satan!' he said. 'You do not have in mind the things of God, but the things of men.'"*

> "He then began to teach them that the Son of Man must suffer many things and be rejected by the elders, chief priests and teachers of the law, and that he must be killed and after three days rise again. He spoke plainly about this..." Mark 8:31-32

3) Jesus's reaction was <u>very strong</u>. Jesus didn't just tell Peter he was <u>wrong</u>, he compared him with <u>Satan</u> tempting Jesus away from his necessary fate.
4) <u>Two</u> more times before entering Jerusalem, Jesus predicted his suffering and death (in Mark 9:30-32 and Mark 10:32-34). On these occasions, the disciples were described as *"<u>afraid</u>"* and *"<u>astonished</u>"*.
5) Modern Christians accept that the passion was an <u>essential</u> part of Jesus's ministry, and that it's through his sacrifice that Christians find <u>salvation</u>.

The Anointing at Bethany Angered the Disciples

1) This is a <u>slightly odd</u> story — it doesn't <u>fit</u> very well with the rest of Jesus's teachings.

> *Jesus Anointed at Bethany* (Mark 14:3-9)
> A few days before his arrest, a woman 'anointed' Jesus by pouring an expensive jar of perfume over him. The disciples *"rebuked her harshly"* for wasting such a valuable thing. It could have been sold for *"more than a year's wages and the money given to the poor"*.
> Jesus's response was unexpected: *"'Leave her alone,' said Jesus... 'She has done a beautiful thing to me. The poor you will always have with you, and you can help them any time you want. But you will not always have me... She poured perfume on my body beforehand to prepare for my burial.'"*

2) 'Messiah' means '<u>anointed one</u>', so some Christians believe she was <u>expressing</u> her faith that Jesus was the Messiah. <u>Kings</u> of Israel were anointed in a similar way, so this could also be a reference to his <u>kingship</u>.
3) Some Christians believe that the disciples' anger showed that they <u>didn't believe</u> Jesus would die — that only <u>Jesus</u> and the <u>woman</u> really understood what was going to happen.
4) But Jesus's response seems surprisingly <u>selfish</u>, particularly given Mark 10:21 (*"Go, sell everything you have and give to the poor..."*).

The Disciple Judas was Part of the Plot to Kill Jesus

1) In Mark 14:1-2, the *"chief priests and the teachers of the law"* plotted to arrest and kill Jesus in *"some sly way"* <u>after</u> the <u>Passover</u> feast. They didn't want to take him in public, because he had too many followers. And not during Passover, because the people might *"riot"*.

> "Then Judas Iscariot, one of the Twelve, went to the chief priests to betray Jesus to them. They... promised to give him money. So he watched for an opportunity to hand him over." Mark 14:10-11

2) One of Jesus's <u>own disciples</u>, Judas Iscariot, decided to betray Jesus to the Jewish authorities.
3) That evening (Mark 14:17-21), Jesus <u>predicted</u> the betrayal:
   "'It is one of the Twelve,' he replied, 'one who dips bread into the bowl with me... But woe to that man who betrays the Son of Man! It would be better for him if he had not been born.'"

Don't bother arguing with him guys — the man's God...

Some Christians interpret Jesus's response at Bethany to be a reference to <u>worship</u>. The woman was showing her <u>complete devotion</u> to Jesus, and the disciples had no right to question her act of worship.

The Last Supper, Judas and the Trial

It's a fairly famous story... you may just know something about this already.

The Last Supper — Jesus Knew he Would be Betrayed

1) The Last Supper (Mark 14:12-26) is the last meal Jesus and the Twelve ate together. They were celebrating the Feast of Unleavened Bread — the first night of the Jewish Passover festival. Passover commemorates the release of the Jews from slavery in Egypt (Exodus 12), and is a very important festival.

2) During the feast, held in the 'upper room' of a man's house, Jesus predicted that one of the disciples would betray him (see previous page). Each disciple denied that it would be him.

3) Jesus then broke a piece of bread and said, "Take it; this is my body." He passed round a cup of wine and said, "This is my blood of the covenant, which is poured out for many".

4) After the supper (Mark 14:25-31) Jesus felt that his death was near, saying "I will not drink again of the fruit of the vine until that day when I drink it anew in the kingdom of God." He then went with the Twelve to the Mount of Olives, where he predicted Peter's denial (see p.27).

> This is a very important passage for modern Christians, as it's the origin of the Eucharist (Holy Communion — see p.14). Many Christians believe that they receive the saving power of Jesus into themselves by eating the bread and drinking the wine at the Eucharist.
>
> Holy Communion also reminds Christians of the 'new covenant' made with God through the death of Jesus.
>
> In Luke 22:19, Jesus adds, "do this in remembrance of me". This phrase isn't part of Mark's Gospel, though, so there's nothing in Mark's account to suggest that Jesus was beginning a tradition.

Jesus Prayed at Gethsemane

1) That night, after the meal, Jesus went with Peter, John and James to the garden of Gethsemane to pray (Mark 14:32-42).

2) Peter, John and James were to keep watch while he prayed, but failed (see p.27).

3) Mark writes that Jesus was "deeply distressed" saying that his soul was "overwhelmed with sorrow to the point of death". Jesus prayed for God to take the "cup" of his suffering from him, but only if that would fit God's plan. Jesus didn't want to die if he didn't have to, but would obey God.

> "'Abba, Father,' he said, 'everything is possible for you. Take this cup from me. Yet not what I will, but what you will.'" Mark 14:36

4) These verses show Jesus's humanity, and so cause problems for some Christians. Some feel that if Jesus was God (as part of the Trinity), then he should know what was necessary, and not question his fate. Others think that, by praying to God, Jesus shows that he's separate from him.

He was Betrayed, Arrested and Tried by the Sanhedrin

1) Judas Iscariot arrived at Gethsemane to betray Jesus (Mark 14:43-52), accompanied by "a crowd armed with swords and clubs, sent from the chief priests, the teachers of the law, and the elders".

2) Judas had arranged a signal with the crowd — the person he kissed was the one they should arrest.

> The betrayal is a thorny subject for Christians. Many believe that Judas's treachery damned him to hell. He betrayed God and sent a good man to his death. But if Jesus's death was necessary for our salvation, then was the betrayal necessary too? And if Judas was destined to be the betrayer, could he have chosen not to be?

3) In Mark 14:53-65, Jesus was put on trial before the High Priest (the leader of the Temple) and the rest of the Sanhedrin (the Jewish supreme council). According to Mark, the court was simply "looking for evidence against Jesus so that they could put him to death".

4) As far as Christians are concerned, this wasn't a real trial, and it had nothing to do with justice. The chief priests felt threatened by Jesus, and this show trial was their opportunity to get rid of him.

5) Various people testified falsely against Jesus, but their stories didn't agree with each other.

6) Jesus stayed silent — he didn't try to defend himself — until the High Priest asked Jesus directly, "Are you the Christ, the Son of the Blessed One?"

> "'I am,' said Jesus. 'And you will see the Son of Man sitting at the right hand of the Mighty One and coming on the clouds of heaven.'" Mark 14:62

7) This was enough to condemn Jesus for the very serious crime of blasphemy — insulting God.

8) Then in the courtyard below, Peter was accused of being a follower of Jesus and denied it three times (see p.27).

The Crucifixion and Resurrection

The Sanhedrin Turned him Over to Pontius Pilate

1) Mark 15:1-15 records the events of the morning after the trial, when Jesus was turned over to Pontius Pilate — the Roman governor of Judea. He had the power to sentence Jesus to death.

2) The priests accused Jesus of *"many things"* before Pilate, but again Jesus refused to answer the accusations. Pilate was *"amazed"*. The one thing Jesus did reply to was Pilate's question: *"Are you the king of the Jews?"* Jesus replied, *"Yes, it is as you say"*.

3) According to Mark, it was customary to release a prisoner to mark Passover, and Pilate asked the crowd if he should release Jesus. The crowd, having been *"stirred up"* by the chief priests, called for a man named Barabbas to be released instead. Barabbas had committed murder in a recent uprising.

4) Mark writes that Pilate knew it was *"out of envy that the chief priests had handed Jesus over to him"*. He writes that the crowd called for Jesus to be crucified, and that Pilate agreed to it to keep the crowd happy.

> *"'Why? What crime has he committed?' asked Pilate. But they shouted all the louder, 'Crucify him!' Wanting to satisfy the crowd, Pilate released Barabbas to them. He had Jesus flogged, and handed him over to be crucified."* Mark 15:14-15

5) So according to Mark, the priests and the Jewish crowd were responsible for Jesus's death, not Pilate. This view was probably influenced by Mark's background. Mark was most likely living in Rome, where Christians were being persecuted by the Roman authorities. He might have felt it wise to paint the Roman Pilate in a good light.

6) Modern Christians tend to lay some of the blame for Jesus's death with Pilate. As a Roman governor, he had the power to refuse to do what the priests wanted, but he chose to go along with them.

Jesus was Crucified and Died at Golgotha

1) Mark 15:21-39 records that Jesus was led to Golgotha (The Place of the Skull) where he was to be crucified — nailed to a cross to hang until he died. Simon of Cyrene carried his cross.

2) Jesus refused the drugged wine he was offered, and was crucified next to two robbers. A sign was fixed to Jesus's cross that read "The King of the Jews", to record the charge against him. Passers-by threw insults at Jesus, saying that he could save others, but couldn't save himself.

3) Christians believe that it was by dying on the cross that Jesus truly saved his followers from death.

4) They believe that God had placed all the sins of the world on Jesus while he hung on the cross. In his suffering, Jesus cried out, *"My God, my God, why have you forsaken me?"*

5) As he died, the curtain of the Temple tore in two. (This would have been a symbol of mourning to the Jews, who ritually tear their clothes when a loved one dies.) A Roman soldier said, *"Surely this man was the Son of God!"*

6) Joseph of Arimathea was allowed to take Jesus's body down from the cross for a decent burial (bodies were usually left on the cross). Joseph placed it in a tomb cut from the rock and rolled a stone over the entrance. Mark implies that this was done in a hurry, because it was getting close to the Sabbath.

Then on the Third Day he was Resurrected

1) As soon as the Sabbath was over, Mark 16:1-8 tells us that Mary Magdalene, Mary the mother of James and Salome went to Jesus's tomb to anoint his body.

2) They got there to find the stone rolled back and the tomb empty. A young man dressed in white was there who told them: *"He has risen! He is not here. See the place where they laid him. But go, tell his disciples and Peter, 'He is going ahead of you into Galilee...'"*

3) The three women fled in terror and didn't say anything to anyone. The oldest copies of Mark end here.

4) Later copies of Mark go on to say that the resurrected Jesus appeared to Mary Magdalene, and then to the eleven remaining apostles. He told them to *"preach the good news to all creation"*.

5) Christians believe that Jesus's resurrection was physical, not just spiritual. The risen Jesus wasn't a ghost — he rose again in the flesh, showing his power over death (see Luke 24:36-49).

The examiners won't be impressed if you don't know this...

Like I said, it's a fairly famous story. But it's not enough to just know what happened — you need to know the significance to Christians of all the events leading up to Jesus's death and resurrection.

Jesus's Baptism and Transfiguration

The start of Jesus's ministry was marked by his baptism by John the Baptist.

Jesus was Baptised by John the Baptist

1) The first few verses of Mark describe the ministry of John the Baptist. John was baptising people in the river Jordan "for the forgiveness of sins". The people confessed their sins and John immersed them in the river to symbolise the sins being washed away.

2) Mark 1:9-11 describes Jesus going to John for baptism. This causes problems for some Christians, since if Jesus was really the son of God and without sin, why did he need to be baptised?

3) But whatever the reason was for him going to John — to encourage his followers to be baptised, or just to mark the start of his ministry — this is where Mark tells us that Jesus was the Son of God.

> "As Jesus was coming up out of the water, he saw heaven being torn open and the Spirit descending on him like a dove. And a voice came from heaven: 'You are my Son, whom I love; with you I am well pleased.'" Mark 1:10-11

Peter Confessed his Faith at Caesarea Philippi

1) 'Confession' in this sense just means acknowledging something — Peter made a statement of belief.

2) In Mark 8:27-33, Jesus and his disciples were travelling towards the city of Caesarea Philippi when Jesus asked them, "Who do you say I am?" Peter replied, "You are the Christ".

3) This was the first time one of Jesus's disciples had openly declared him to be the Christ or Messiah (see p.35). Jesus told them not to tell anyone who he was (this is often called the Messianic Secret).

Matthew's Account of Peter's Confession is Important for Roman Catholics (16:13-20)

In Matthew, Jesus responds to Peter's confession by offering him the "keys of the kingdom of heaven":

For Roman Catholics, this passage marks the foundation of their Church, with Peter as the first Pope (Bishop of Rome).

> "Blessed are you, Simon son of Jonah... I tell you that you are Peter, and on this rock I will build my church, and the gates of Hades will not overcome it. I will give you the keys of the kingdom of heaven; whatever you bind on earth will be bound in heaven, and whatever you loose on earth will be loosed in heaven." Matthew 16:17-19

'Peter' means 'rock' in Greek.

Mark's account of the event doesn't include any mention of this, so Matthew's record is more important for Roman Catholic Christians today.

Jesus Met with Elijah and Moses at his Transfiguration

1) Mark 9:1-10 describes a miraculous event called the transfiguration, in which Jesus's appearance changed in front of Peter, John and James.

> "...he was transfigured before them. His clothes became dazzling white..." Mark 9:2-3

2) The prophets Moses and Elijah appeared, and were talking to Jesus. Elijah is the Old Testament prophet who is prophesied to return before the Messiah.

3) This is the most openly 'god-like' thing that Jesus is recorded as having done in Mark's Gospel. Some Christians are uneasy about it — they find it hard to reconcile Jesus the man with this sort of transformation.

4) While the disciples stood there terrified, a cloud came down and enveloped them. A voice from the cloud said, "This is my Son, whom I love. Listen to him!", and then everything returned to normal.

5) As at the baptism, this is the voice of God himself declaring Jesus to be his son.

6) Jesus again told Peter, James and John not to tell anyone what they'd seen until after he'd risen from the dead.

7) But if Peter, James and John had witnessed this transfiguration, seen the prophets, and heard the voice of God, it's hard to understand why they struggled to accept the idea of Jesus's resurrection (Mark 16:11-12).

The clues are there — as we go throoooough the Gospel...

So the big question in these pages is, 'who exactly was this Jesus chappy?' The stuff on this page seems to point quite firmly to Jesus being the Messiah, the Son of God. But Jesus never actually says so until his trial.

Jesus's Miracles

According to Mark's Gospel, Jesus performed many <u>miracles</u>. These miracles showed that he had <u>God's power</u>, but they also demonstrated the importance of <u>faith</u>.

Healing Miracles and Faith are Linked

Jesus exercised his own faith every time he performed a <u>miracle</u>. And he showed that people could be cured miraculously of both physical and mental illness — as long as they had <u>faith</u>.

> ### The Raising of Jairus's Daughter (Mark 5:21-43)
> Jairus, a synagogue ruler, begged Jesus to heal his daughter. When Jesus arrived, the girl was apparently dead already, but Jesus revived her. As in most of the healing miracles, faith is <u>crucial</u>. The sick girl's <u>father</u> demonstrated faith by asking Jesus for help.

"Jesus told the synagogue ruler, 'Don't be afraid; just believe.'" Mark 5:36

> ### The Healing of a Man with Evil Spirits (Mark 5:1-20)
> A man was possessed by many evil spirits that caused him to hurt himself: *"he would cry out and cut himself with stones"*. The spirits were so strong that the man could break the chains put on his wrists and ankles. The man <u>ran</u> to Jesus and fell on his <u>knees</u> in front of him, but the <u>demons</u> spoke through the man. They called Jesus *"Son of the Most High God"* and referred to themselves as *"Legion... for we are many"*. The demons begged Jesus to send them into a herd of pigs, rather than driving them from the country altogether. When the demons entered the 2000 pigs, they ran to the lake and drowned. Jesus told the man to spread the word about what he had done.

Mark never tells us the <u>name</u> of the man, but you'll often hear him called "<u>Legion</u>" after the demons that possessed him.

1) There are two ways of looking at these <u>healing miracle</u> stories — either as <u>descriptions</u> of real events, or as <u>symbolic</u> of Christian teachings.

2) Where the miracles seem to be treating what we'd now consider <u>mental illness</u> (e.g. Legion), most Christians see how <u>faith</u> could have a <u>profound</u> effect. But healing <u>physical illness</u>, or even <u>death</u>, through faith alone is <u>harder</u> for some modern Christians to accept.

3) Many Christians believe that the story of Legion is <u>symbolic</u>, where the man represents the whole of <u>humanity</u> being plagued by the many demons of <u>sin</u>.

Jesus Controlled Nature — Inspiring Awe and Wonder

Mark also describes several <u>nature miracles</u>, in which Jesus shows his <u>power</u> over nature.

> ### Calming the storm (Mark 4:35-41)
> A storm broke out and threatened to sink the boat that Jesus and the disciples were in. Jesus calmly instructed the wind to die down, which it did. The disciples were filled with awe at what they saw: *"They were terrified and asked each other, 'Who is this? Even the wind and the waves obey him!'"*

> ### Walking on water (Mark 6:45-52)
> Jesus caught up with his disciples' boat by walking across the water. Although they'd just seen him feed the 5000, they were still shocked at his powers.

> ### Feeding the 5000 (Mark 6:32-44)
> A crowd had gathered around Jesus and the disciples, but there were only 5 loaves and 2 fish to eat. Jesus gave thanks to God, broke the bread and the disciples passed the food round. All 5000 people had enough to eat, and there was enough food left over to fill 12 baskets.

"Then he climbed into the boat with them... They were completely amazed, for they had not understood about the loaves; their hearts were hardened." Mark 6:51-52

1) Taken at <u>face value</u>, these stories cause <u>problems</u> for some modern Christians.

2) In a world that follows the normal physical laws, you <u>can't</u> turn 5 loaves and 2 fish into enough food to feed thousands of people, or walk on water as though it was solid ground.

3) Some Christians believe that <u>physical laws</u> didn't bind Jesus, because he was the <u>Son of God</u>, and had God's <u>power</u> within him. Others prefer to view the stories <u>symbolically</u>. For example, the feeding of the five thousand can be seen to represent God <u>providing</u> for those who <u>trust</u> and have <u>faith</u> in him.

You won't need a miracle if you learn this stuff properly...

In the story of Legion, the demons call Jesus the "Son of the Most High God". So Mark describes the demons as recognising Jesus for who he was, even if the people he was ministering to didn't.

The Titles of Jesus

In Mark's Gospel, Jesus is called by a number of <u>titles</u>, each of which gives a clue as to Jesus's <u>identity</u>.

His <u>Followers</u> Called Jesus the Messiah

1) The words '<u>Messiah</u>' in Hebrew, and '<u>Christ</u>' in Greek, both mean '<u>anointed one</u>'.
2) They come from the practice of <u>consecrating</u> kings and priests to God by anointing them with blessed oil.
3) In the Jewish scriptures, the Messiah is the promised <u>King of Israel</u> who will deliver the Jews from suffering, and usher in the 'messianic age' — an age of peace when everyone will worship God.
4) Christians believe that <u>Jesus</u> was the Messiah promised in the books of Isaiah and Zechariah.
5) The Gospels pick out events and actions that show Jesus <u>fulfilling</u> many of the messianic <u>prophecies</u> during his time on Earth. There aren't many examples of this in Mark's Gospel, but there are lots in Matthew, e.g. Matthew 21:5 describes the <u>Triumphal Entry</u> (see p.29) as a fulfilment of Zechariah 9:9.
6) Christians believe that, during his life, Jesus only fulfilled <u>some</u> of the prophecies about the Messiah. And that he will <u>return</u> (the Second Coming) to bring in the <u>messianic age</u>, or the <u>Kingdom of God</u>.

Jesus <u>Called</u> Himself the Son of Man

1) When Jesus refers to <u>himself</u> in Mark's Gospel, he uses the title '<u>Son of Man</u>', e.g.

- healing the <u>paralysed man</u> (see p.28): *"...the Son of Man has authority on earth to forgive sins..."*
- in response to the request of <u>James and John</u> to sit at his side in glory (see p.27): *"...the Son of Man did not come to be served, but to serve..."*
- the prediction of his <u>passion</u> (see p.30): *"...the Son of Man must suffer many things...".*
- at his <u>trial</u> before the Sanhedrin (see p.31): *"...you will see the Son of Man sitting at the right hand of the Mighty One and coming on the clouds of heaven."*

2) Many Christians see the title as a reference to Jesus's <u>humanity</u>. They believe that he lived, suffered and died as a <u>man</u>.
3) As a human, Jesus could <u>atone</u> for the sins of humanity (p.3-4).
4) It's likely that the title was also a reference to the prophet <u>Daniel</u>:

"In my vision... there before me was one like a son of man, coming with the clouds of heaven... He was given authority, glory and sovereign power... His dominion is an everlasting dominion that will not pass away..." Daniel 7:13-14

Christians <u>Believe</u> Jesus is the Son of God

1) Christians believe that Jesus is the second person of the Trinity (see p.3) and the <u>Son of God</u>.
2) There's <u>evidence</u> for this in Mark's Gospel:

The clearest evidence comes from Jesus's <u>baptism</u> and <u>transfiguration</u>, where the voice of God declared Jesus to be his <u>Son</u> (see p.33).

Jesus prayed to God as his "<u>Father</u>".

Jesus's <u>miracles</u> (see previous page) showed that he had the power of God.

Jesus confirmed that he was the Son of God at his <u>trial</u> before the <u>Sanhedrin</u> (see p.31).

Jesus rose from the <u>dead</u> (see p.32) — demonstrating his divinity.

3) But <u>not everyone</u> is convinced from Mark's account that Jesus was divine. He showed normal, human <u>emotions</u> at Gethsemane (see p.31), and up until his trial, he never <u>claimed</u> to be the Son of God.
4) Others don't <u>trust</u> the evidence of Mark's Gospel. It was probably written some time <u>after</u> Jesus's death, by someone who wasn't a <u>first-hand witness</u> of the things he's describing.

Son of Man — or Son of God...

No <u>person</u> called Jesus the Son of God until his trial, because <u>connecting</u> yourself with God in that way was considered blasphemous by the Jews. But if you believe Mark's account, a supernatural voice said it twice.

Practice Questions

Oooh... lots of questions. And I know what you're thinking — "I could just... skip... it." But there's NO WAY you could possibly remember everything first time through, so use these questions to fill in the gaps...

1) **What is/are:**
   a) a disciple?
   b) the kingdom?
   c) the commandments?
   d) Peter's denial?

   e) the Law?
   f) fasting?
   g) corban?
   h) ritual cleanliness?

   i) the Sabbath?
   j) Gethsemane?
   k) Golgotha?
   l) the Sanhedrin?

   To get the 2 marks for these questions you just have to learn the key terms.

   Who was/were:
   m) Levi?
   n) the Sons of Zebedee?
   o) the Pharisees?

   p) the scribes?
   q) the Sadducees?
   r) Pontius Pilate?

   s) John the Baptist?
   t) Elijah?
   u) Jairus?

2) **For each of the following questions, give two reasons for your point of view.**
   a) Do you think Jesus was right to call Levi as a disciple?
   b) Do you think Christians should serve others?
   c) Do you think Christians should keep the Sabbath?
   d) Do you think the woman at Bethany was right to anoint Jesus with perfume?
   e) Do you think Pontius Pilate was responsible for Jesus's death?
   f) Do you think Jesus was the Messiah?

   Your marks here come from the reasons you use to back up your opinion. Each of these questions is worth 4 marks in the exam.

3) **For these questions, take extra care with your spelling, punctuation and grammar, and express yourself as clearly as possible.**
   a) Explain why the calling and sending out of the first disciples is important to Christians today.
   b) Explain why Jesus's teachings about true family might cause problems for some Christians today.
   c) Explain why the healing of the paralysed man led to conflict.
   d) Explain the significance to modern Christians of Jesus's disagreements with the Jews over the meaning of the Law.
   e) Explain why the Last Supper is important to Christians.
   f) Explain the significance of Jesus's death and resurrection to Christians.
   g) Explain why Matthew's account of Peter's confession at Caesarea Philippi is important to Roman Catholics.
   h) Explain why Jesus's healing miracles might cause problems for some Christians today.

   These are the big 8-mark ones — so they're worth taking a little bit of time over. And don't forget your spelling, punctuation and grammar.

4) **Read the following statements:**
   a) "The disciples failed Jesus."
   b) "Helping people is more important than religious traditions."
   c) "Judas was evil."
   d) "Jesus rose from the dead."
   e) "Jesus fed 5000 people with 5 loaves and 2 fishes."
   f) "Jesus was the Son of God."

   For each statement:
   (i) Do you agree? Give reasons for your opinion.
   (ii) Give reasons why some people may disagree with you.

   In your answers you should refer to Mark's Gospel and Christianity.

   This lot of questions should remind you that you need to learn both sides of the big arguments — no matter how passionately you believe in your own opinion. 3 marks for your opinion — 3 marks for someone else's.

Do Well in Your Exam

You've learnt all the <u>facts</u> — now it's time to get those <u>grades</u>.

You'll have a 1½ Hour Exam

1) For the Christianity or Roman Catholicism exam you'll have to answer a question on <u>each</u> of the <u>four topics</u> — <u>Beliefs and Values</u>, <u>Community and Tradition</u>, <u>Worship and Celebration</u>, and <u>Living the Christian Life</u>.

2) For Mark's Gospel, you'll have a similar exam, but your topics will be <u>Discipleship</u>, <u>Conflict and Argument</u>, <u>Death and Resurrection</u> and <u>The Identity of Jesus</u>.

3) For each topic you'll have the choice of <u>two questions</u>. Each question is worth <u>20 marks</u> and will be split into <u>four parts</u>. You'll have to answer <u>all four parts</u> of each question you choose.

4) For part (<u>c</u>) of each question, you'll be marked in part on your <u>use of English</u> — this means you need to use top quality <u>spelling</u>, <u>punctuation</u> and <u>grammar</u> — and proper <u>formal</u> language. Don't forget to use all the <u>fancy words</u> that you've learned during the course.

There are Easy Marks for Knowing What Things Mean

Two marks out of each question are for just knowing what the <u>important terms mean</u>. These questions don't carry a lot of marks, so keep your answers <u>short</u> and <u>to the point</u> — but make sure you define the term <u>properly</u>. Learn the terms that relate to your unit from the glossary.

> a) What is meant by **displaying religion**? (2 marks)

Carrying out religious duties in public to impress other people rather than God.

Try to answer this kind of question in one sentence.

This is too long. You <u>don't have</u> <u>time</u> to write an essay on questions that don't offer many marks. Keep your answer short and to the point.

In the Sermon on the Mount, Jesus says that we are to carry out acts of charity and worship in private, rather than in public. He says that praying loudly on street corners, or making sure people know when we give to charity is wrong, because we should be doing it for the benefit of God rather than an audience. We describe this fault as displaying religion.

But this is just an example, not a definition, so it'd only get you 1 mark.

Praying in public.

You'll be asked about What you Think

There's <u>no right answer</u> to this kind of question — only <u>good answers</u> that'll get you <u>lots of marks</u> and <u>bad answers</u> that <u>won't</u>. The difference between the two is that good answers give <u>clearly developed reasons</u>. You can make reference to the <u>religious teachings</u> you have studied, but in part (<u>b</u>) you <u>don't have to</u>.

> b) Do you think that the contemplative life is a worthwhile vocation?
> Give two reasons for your point of view. (4 marks)

I do not believe that the contemplative life is worthwhile because I believe that all Christians should play a role in evangelising, which you cannot do from behind monastery walls.
I also believe that those living the active life can better fulfil Jesus's orders that we help those in need, while still devoting their lives to God.

Both of these answers are pretty good, despite arguing different things from different perspectives.

Make sure you back up each point with a relevant reason.

Try to use proper sentences. You won't get extra marks for it on this question — but it'll make it easier for the person marking your paper.

I believe that taking up the contemplative life is a very worthwhile choice, as it is the only way that a person can fully commit themselves to a life of prayer — which is the best way of getting to know God.
Religious communities living the contemplative life have been around for centuries. If the life they lived there was not fruitful, those orders that stay enclosed would have died away by now.

Try contemplating this page for a while...

Don't forget — you don't get marks for what you believe, only for the reasons you give to back up your opinions.

Do Well in Your Exam

More stuff for you on the <u>exam</u> right here. Get <u>stuck in</u>.

You'll have to Explain Why...

1) For the part (<u>c</u>) question, you'll get some marks for the <u>quality</u> of your <u>written English</u>. This includes your <u>spelling</u>, <u>punctuation</u> and <u>grammar</u>.

2) You'll also get marks for using the kind of <u>fancy words</u> that you'll find in the <u>glossary</u> — learn what they <u>mean</u>, how to <u>use</u> them, and how to <u>spell</u> them.

Best break out the best handwriting for this one.

---

c) Explain why most Christians believe they should help the poor. (8 marks)

> Jesus explains to his followers in the Sermon on the Mount that the most important thing is to "<u>do to others what you would have them do to you</u>." This means that Christians have to <u>help the poor</u>, because if we were <u>in their shoes</u> we would want help ourselves.
>
> Jesus also tells us in the book of Matthew that those who <u>feed the hungry</u> and who <u>give clothes to those who need them</u> are in effect, giving those things to Jesus himself: "<u>whatever you did for one of the least of these brothers of mine, you did for me.</u>" Jesus tells us that it is those people who help others in need who will be saved. That means that, for Christians, helping people is <u>necessary</u> for their <u>salvation</u>.

It won't hurt if you remember a little bit of scripture.

Some Christian teaching — like the Golden Rule — can be useful in lots of different contexts.

3) If you <u>structure</u> your answer well you'll get more marks — so <u>sketch</u> out a <u>plan</u> before you write your answer.

4) The best marks will go to those who put in a <u>number</u> of reasons and/or <u>develop</u> their reasons well.

5) To get top marks you usually have to give either '<u>four brief</u> reasons, <u>three</u> reasons with one <u>developed</u>, <u>two developed</u> reasons or a <u>comprehensive</u> explanation using one reason only'. So if you've only got one point to make in an answer like this, you'd better make sure you know it inside out. (The answer above gives two developed reasons.)

---

c) Explain why the parable of the tenants is important for Christians today. (8 marks)

> In the parable of the tenants, Jesus teaches about how the <u>old religious authorities</u> (the tenants) would be replaced by those who <u>truly sought</u> God's will (the new tenants).
>
> The parable serves as a warning that only those who do God's will will be <u>rewarded</u>, and that those who <u>stand against</u> his will cannot continue to do so for ever. This may be important for Christians today who feel that they are doing wrong. They should cease because in the end <u>there will be judgement</u>. For Christians who are suffering injustice it could suggest that they should be patient as <u>justice will come</u> in the end.
>
> The parable of the tenants is perhaps most important for Christians today as it shows that being a disciple is a <u>difficult and dangerous</u> thing. Simply being a Christian has been dangerous at many times in history, and is still <u>not a safe option</u> in some places in the world.

It can be good to put your best point last.

Thou shalt write clearly...

As much as you may know every little fact that pops up in this book, a large chunk of how well you do in the exam will come down to, well... how good you are at exams. Make sure you spend enough time reading through these pages, and enough time practising doing exam-style questions under timed conditions. It'll all pay off in the end.

Do Well in Your Exam

Here's a page on those pesky questions where you have to understand other people's opinions.

You need to know Both Sides of the Argument

1) In part (d) you'll get the same marks for writing what you think and for writing what people who disagree with you think. So spend the same time and effort on each.

2) You'll be told to refer to Christianity, Roman Catholicism or the Gospel of Mark here, so make sure you do. If you don't do this in at least one part of your answer, you can only score a maximum of half marks.

---

d) "Christmas is one of the most important days of the year for Christians."
   In your answer you should refer to Christianity.
   (i) Do you agree? Give reasons for your opinion.   (3 marks)
   (ii) Give reasons why some people may disagree with you.   (3 marks)

(i) I believe that Christmas should be treated as one of the most important dates in the Christian calendar as it celebrates the incarnation — the birth of Jesus.

While we do not know the specific date on which Jesus was born, it seems right to take one day out of every year to celebrate it. In the UK, the date of 25th December has been accepted for centuries, and so has become a tradition that reminds people of Jesus.

(ii) People who do not believe in the importance of Christmas argue that whatever value it had has been lost, since the festival has become more about giving expensive presents and less about religious observance.

Christians might argue that the importance of Christmas should not be anywhere near that of Easter — the only truly important Christian festival. Easter celebrates the most important point in the story of Jesus for Christians — his resurrection.

> **Try to make the reasons why people disagree with you as good as the reasons for your own opinion.**

(i) I would argue that Christmas should not be regarded as an important day in the Christian calendar as it is not mentioned anywhere in the New Testament that the early Christians celebrated Christ's birthday. As such, there does not seem to be any real reason to accept Christmas as a genuinely Christian festival.

In fact there are many elements of the celebration of Christmas that reflect pre-Christian and pagan traditions rather than specifically Christian ones. Examples of this include the bringing of 'Christmas' trees into the house and the date, which reflects a pagan winter festival.

(ii) Some Christians might argue that, as an opportunity for people to get together with their families, Christmas represents a vitally important day in the calendar of modern Christians. Families are important for Christians, and Christmas is often a time when we can be with our parents (one of the commandments is to "honour your father and mother"). It is also a special time of year for children. In the Gospel of Mark, Jesus tells his followers "anyone who will not receive the kingdom of God like a little child will never enter it."

> **Don't waffle. If you keep your answer more to the point, you'll get more in. And that means more marks.**

> **If you can only think of one reason in the exam, make sure you develop it as best you can.**

Don't forget the Basics

1) Read the questions carefully. Make sure you read both questions on each topic before you pick one of them. Remember, you've got to answer all the parts of the questions you pick.

2) Be aware of how much time you're using. If you've got a bit left at the end read through your answers.

"I think exams are rubbish" — "I think exams are great..."

...but that's just because they pay me to put revision guides together. Make sure you learn the different arguments for both sides of the key issues. It's not a bad lesson to take away from the exam — even if you believe something strongly, it's worthwhile knowing why other people don't. You might even change your mind...

Glossary: Christianity & Roman Catholicism

The green definitions are for Christianity only. The purple ones are for Roman Catholicism only.

absolution	Forgiveness of sins granted by God through a priest, following confession and penance.
active life	The life lived by members of a religious order who work 'in the world' as well as praying.
Advent	The month leading up to Christmas, during which many Christians prepare themselves spiritually for the Second Coming of Christ.
Anglican Churches	Churches that are in communion with the Church of England (they agree with the Church of England on matters of doctrine).
apostolic	A belief that the Church was founded by, and receives its authority from, Jesus's Apostles.
atonement	Reconciliation with God. This often refers to Jesus's sacrifice on the cross to pay for our sin.
believer's baptism	The baptism of a person who is old enough to understand what it means to become a Christian and who has chosen the faith for his- or herself.
bishops	Priests who have been chosen to have responsibility for all the churches in a diocese. Roman Catholic bishops are appointed by the Pope.
catechism	A series of statements laying down the official teachings of the Roman Catholic Church.
catholic	Universal. Used to describe the community of all Christian believers.
celibacy	Not taking part in any sexual activities.
charismatic worship	Worship involving spiritual gifts and experiences, such as 'speaking in tongues' (unknown languages), shaking or crying uncontrollably.
charity	Freely giving money, time or some other kind of help to someone in need.
chrism	The blessed oil used in the sacraments of confirmation and ordination.
commemoration	The belief that the Eucharist recalls and re-enacts the Last Supper, but that the bread and wine do not physically become the flesh and blood of Jesus.
compassion	A feeling of pity for, and desire to help, those who are suffering.
confirmation	The sacrament in which a Christian (who is old enough to understand what it means to be a Christian) renews the promises made on their behalf at baptism.
contemplative life	The life lived by members of a religious order who devote themselves to prayer and study.
contrition	Feeling genuinely sorry for committing a sin and determining not to sin again.
creeds	Statements of religious beliefs.
displaying religion	Making a show of good deeds or religious observance to impress other people, e.g. praying in the street.
Eucharist	The sacrament of Holy Communion, in which a believer receives blessed bread and wine.
the evangelical counsels	The three vows taken by members of religious orders — poverty, chastity and obedience.
faith	Firmly-held belief without (and without need for) logical proof.
holy	Sacred, or belonging to God.
holy orders	Ordination to a deacon, priest or bishop.
Holy Week	The last week of Lent, lasting from Palm Sunday until the day before Easter Sunday.
hypocrite	A person who act out beliefs they don't really hold, or whose actions don't match what they say.
incarnation	The act by which Christians believe God became human, in the form of Jesus.
laity	All non-ordained members of the Church — those who aren't bishops, priests or deacons.

Glossary: Christianity & Roman Catholicism

Law of Moses	The Jewish laws handed down to Moses by God.
Lent	The 40 days leading up to Easter, which commemorate the 40 days and nights Jesus spent in the wilderness after his baptism.
liturgy of the Eucharist	A series of prayers and rituals in which the Last Supper is re-enacted, during which Roman Catholics believe that the bread and wine of Holy Communion are transubstantiated into the flesh and blood of Christ.
liturgy of the word	The second part of the Mass — a series of Bible readings, a short sermon and a recitation of the creed.
Magisterium	The ability and authority of the Pope and bishops to correctly interpret the Bible, and to teach on matters of faith and morals.
Mass	The Roman Catholic service that includes the Eucharist.
monastic life	The life lived by monks or nuns in enclosed religious communities.
monotheism	A belief in one god.
New Testament	The part of the Bible covering the life and teachings of Jesus and the early Christian Church.
Nonconformist Churches	Protestant Churches that aren't part of the Anglican Communion.
non-liturgical worship	Worship that doesn't use set forms of words and rituals.
Old Testament	The part of the Bible containing the Jewish books of laws, histories, prophecies, etc.
ordination	The sacrament of holy orders, by which someone is made a deacon, priest or bishop.
Orthodox Churches	Churches who recognise the authority of the Patriarch of Constantinople.
papacy	The office of the Pope.
penance	A number of prayers to be said or an action to be carried out in order to show contrition.
penitential rite	The first part of the Mass — this is a joint confession of sin and a request for God's forgiveness and mercy in the form of the 'Kyrie' prayer.
real presence	The Protestant belief that the bread and wine of the Eucharist contain the presence of Jesus (but don't become his flesh and blood).
religious community	A religious order in which everyone lives together, e.g. in a monastery.
repentance	Being sorry for our sins and trying hard not to repeat them.
rite of communion	Receiving the body and blood of Christ at the Eucharist.
sacrament	A ceremony, or outward sign, of the direct communication of God's saving grace.
salvation	The act of saving from sin and death.
Sermon on the Mount	A summary of Jesus's teachings on how to live a Christian life — Matthew 5-7.
transubstantiation	The physical transformation of the bread and wine of the Eucharist into the flesh and blood of Christ (in all but appearance).
Trinity	The Christian belief that God exists as three in one — the Father, the Son and the Holy Spirit.
Unity	The Christian belief in God as one supreme being.
Virgin Birth	The Christian belief that Jesus was born of a virgin — that Mary became pregnant through the influence of the Holy Spirit.
vocation	A call from God to lead a Christian life, or someone's 'calling in life'.

Glossary: Mark's Gospel

baptism	Confessing and 'washing away' of sins by immersion in water.
blasphemy	Insulting God.
confession	Acknowledging something. In the case of Peter at Caesarea Philippi, acknowledging faith.
corban	A gift dedicated to God (and so not usable for anything else).
crucifixion	Death by being nailed to a cross — the method of Jesus's execution.
disciples	Followers of Jesus. This can refer to just his followers in the Bible or to all Christians.
Elijah	The Old Testament prophet who is prophesied to return before the Messiah.
the eye of a needle	Part of a metaphor for how hard it is for the rich to enter the Kingdom of God.
Feast of Unleavened Bread	The first night of the Jewish Passover festival.
Gethsemane	The garden where Jesus prayed before his arrest.
Golgotha	The 'place of the skull' where Jesus was crucified.
healing miracle	A miracle in which Jesus healed physical or mental illness through the power of faith.
Jairus	A synagogue ruler whose daughter was brought back to life by Jesus.
John the Baptist	A preacher who baptised Jesus (and others) in the river Jordan before Jesus started teaching.
Judas Iscariot	The disciple who betrayed Jesus to the authorities.
the kingdom	The rulership of God in people's lives.
Last Supper	Jesus's final meal — a celebration of Passover with his disciples. The origin of the Eucharist.
the Law	The Jewish laws of the Torah, handed down by God.
Legion	Many evil spirits who possessed a man, and were driven out into a herd of pigs.
Levi	A tax collector who was called to be one of Jesus's disciples.
Messiah	The 'anointed one' — a prophesied saviour who would bring in the Kingdom of God.
Moses	The Old Testament prophet to whom God revealed the Law.
nature miracle	A miracle in which Jesus demonstrates his power over nature, e.g. walking on the water.
Palm Sunday	The day of Jesus's Triumphal Entry into Jerusalem (or the festival commemorating that day).
Passion	The sufferings of Jesus in the time leading up to his death.
Passover	The Jewish festival celebrating the Jews' release from slavery in Egypt.
Peter's denial	Peter denying that he knew Jesus after Jesus's trial by the Sanhedrin.
Pharisees	A Jewish group who studied the Law and were dedicated to keeping the Jewish faith alive.
Pontius Pilate	The Roman governor of Judea who sentenced Jesus to death.
ritual cleanliness	Laws on food and washing that prevented anything spiritually 'unclean' entering a Jew's body.
Sabbath	The Jewish day of rest (Saturday).
Sadducees	A group of priests who ran the Temple in Jerusalem and believed in sticking rigidly to the Torah.
Sanhedrin	The supreme Jewish council, who tried Jesus for blasphemy.
scribes	Religious lawyers who made copies of the Torah, and so knew it very well.
self-sacrifice	Putting other people's needs before your own.
service	Doing something for someone else — providing assistance or care.
Son of Man	The title Jesus uses to refer to himself in Mark's Gospel.
Sons of Zebedee	John and James, two of the first disciples to be called.
the Temple	The building in Jerusalem where sacrifices (e.g. burnt offerings) were made to God.
transfiguration	An event in which Jesus's appearance changed miraculously, making his clothes 'dazzling white'.
true family	Jesus's teaching that a disciple's true family are his fellow disciples, not his blood relatives.
true greatness	Jesus's teaching that greatness in the eyes of God comes from serving others.
the Twelve	The twelve disciples chosen as Apostles — Jesus's closest followers.
upper room	The place where Jesus and his disciples ate the Last Supper.

Index

Index